ISBN 978-1-61808-126-1

Printed in the United States of America

White Feather Press

Reaffirming Faith in God, Family, and Country!

High Praise for Denny Gillem and *The Smiling Ranger*!

"This is a fascinating book, filled with concise and very insightful stories. It is VERY readable!"

–Captain Paul J Ryan, US Navy (Retired)

""I was thinking about" is another way of saying "I got a war story, no shit, listen to this." Ranger Denny Gillem details his life through the 1960s, 70s and early 80s. He refreshingly explains the characters of the best Americans that live and sacrifice for our nation. LTC Gillem's memories provide a view of military life with patriots in combat and details explaining the challenges and hysterical side of military life with family in a long successful career culminating in life after the military to eventually carry on the message on a "radio show" of how our Patriot warriors in the military continue to provide the "Freedom" we hold so dear.

–CSM Douglas Greenway, US Army Ranger (Retired)

"One perception of the military is that it's an overly disciplined, regimented, and humorless institution. Denny Gillem's insightful book *The Smiling Ranger* provides an alternative view. It's a nostalgic compilation of memorable vignettes that depict the free spirit, independence, and humor of life in the military. It confirms for those who serve that the military is, first and foremost, memorable memories of friendships and adventures."

– Major General John Admire USMC (Retired)

"Denny Gillem's, the *The Smiling Ranger* is fast paced and a delight to read. The book is informative and captures the life of one of America's highly decorated Veterans from childhood through his Army career and today as a patriotic talk show host. I enjoyed it and recommend it."

–Major General Paul Mock, US Army (Retired)

Acknowledgements and Thanks

About a year ago, two of my co-hosts, Josh Leng and Skip Coryell began leaning on me to write a book. I had been using funny stories from my career on the show for years. Thus their encouragement caused my sense of humor and my hunger to write to "crank up." So I salute Josh and Skip as my motivators. I salute my amazing wife of almost 49 years Marilyn for her encouragement and support as I wrote and wrote and wrote—she's also a great editor.

Once I started writing it was Skip Coryell who prodded and mentored me and edited my comments—and formatted the book. Without his vision, skills, and leadership there would be no *Smiling Ranger*.

I must also acknowledge all the wonderful leaders who taught me how to be a soldier over the years. How can I not include the man who was my company's Tactical Officer at West Point and who was my battalion commander when we deployed the 101st Airborne Division to fight in Vietnam, Brigadier General Richard Tallman; General Tallman was killed in action in Vietnam. And then there was my first sergeant in the 101st Airborne, Sergeant Major (Ret) Robert Cook. Top retired and became a pastor; he went home to be with his Lord a number of years ago. These two soldiers are at the top of my memory as I think of my career—there are thousands of others to whom I also owe thanks.

Finally, I acknowledge the Lord my God who has given me such a wonderful life and even the ability to write about parts of it.

Dedication

This book is dedicated to my wonderful wife Marilyn and our son Dave—they lived most of this book with me. It's also dedicated to the thousands of men and women with whom I served during my 22 years on active duty in the US Army—it was a great honor to serve with them.

The Smiling Ranger

The life and career of an army ranger

by
Lieutenant Colonel
Denny Gillem

Host of America's #1 military and veteran's
radio show "Frontlines of Freedom!"

In My Youth

I'M A **CALIFORNIA BOY;** I'M THE OLD-
est of 4 children—and the only boy. While no one in
my direct line (that I know of) ever served in the military, I knew that I wanted to be in the Army for most of my
youth. I took Army Junior ROTC in high school and applied
for West Point before graduation. Unfortunately, my grades
were less than stellar, so I didn't get an appointment until my
third try.

I went to the local Junior College for a year and had a dis-
astrous second semester. I then went to New Mexico Military
Institute, a military high school and junior college; there I got
my academic act together. I entered the US Military Academy
on 5 July 1960. I graduated in June 1964—at the very top, of
the bottom third, of the class.

Upon graduation I received my first choice of branches. I
became an infantryman. After graduation leave, I was off to
Fort Benning, GA (also known as Fort Beginning or Benning
School for Boys) for Airborne and Ranger Schools. The
next stop, my first assignment with troops, was Fort Carson,
Colorado. My career was off and running.

After a few months at Fort Carson I volunteered to serve
in Vietnam, then I met a young lady and got engaged. After
a year in Vietnam I came home to get married and to join
the 101st Airborne Division at Fort Campbell, KY—where, a

year later, we deployed to Vietnam. I came home from this second tour highly decorated, selected for an early promotion to major—and went on to have a normal, fun, fulfilling career. I retired in 1986 in Grand Rapids, MI. I loved every minute I was in the Army (well, maybe not every minute), and I was ready to retire when I did.

I've always had a pretty good sense of humor and a mostly-positive outlook on life. I'd like to share some of my thoughts and experiences with you—some serious, most not-so. Actually, many of these stories have already been shared on the air. My weekly, syndicated, military talk-radio show, *Frontlines of Freedom* is my passion, and over the past 8 years, I've shared many of these stories—that's why most of them begin with "I was thinking…" because this is how I shared them with my co-hosts and listeners. Here's hoping you enjoy reading them as much as I did living them.

I was thinking about...

the fact that I started kindergarten when I was four years old, so I was always the youngest one in my class. I was also quite tall, so I looked older than I really was. As a result, my parents let me start driving when my high school classmates did. (Legally you could get a driver's license back then when you turned 16.) I started driving at 15. I was also very active in my high school Junior ROTC unit. One thing our unit had, and I lead, was an honor guard; we'd fire a 21-round salute at military funerals. The weapon we used as cadets was the M-1 rifle, so that's what the honor guard used.

On one occasion there was a funeral on Saturday. Rather than find a way to come in on Saturday morning (when the school was closed) on Friday afternoon I just took seven M-1s and put them in my trunk, along with a box of blank cartridges. That evening I was on my way to see a friend when I was stopped by the police for failing to yield the right-of-way while making a left turn. I was very nervous at being stopped because, one, I had never been stopped before; two, because I was driving alone with only a learner's permit (which required

I be driving with a licensed driver), and, three, because I had a trunk full of military rifles. I did get a ticket and couldn't drive my car anywhere as I had no driver's license. I called a friend who came and drove my car home for me. Ultimately, I had to pay a fine; all things considered, I got off really easy.

The M1 Garand Rifle

General George S. Patton called it "the greatest implement of battle ever devised."

Designed by John C. Garand in 1928, the M1 Rifle was the US military service rifle from 1936 to 1957. Approximately 6.25 million Garand rifles were produced.

Known for it's 8-round en-bloc clip, internal magazine which gave off a distinctive "ping" sound when empty.

Chambered for the .30-06 Springfield rifle cartridge, the Garand was the first standard-issue semi-automatic rifle.

I was remembering that...

after really messing up academically during my first year at Junior College I enrolled at New Mexico Military Institute (NMMI) in Roswell, NM. My goal was to get focused and get my academics back to where they should be. We lived in barracks and wore uniforms everywhere; it was the environment I needed. Our barracks was a hollow square with all cadet rooms entered from the inside of the square; we had formations in the center of the square. One of my classmates was from Hawaii. He made it clear that he'd never been in snow and was nervous about walking and moving in it. Of course it snowed that winter, and the first morning that we had snow a bunch of us charged in his room, grabbed him (he was in his underwear) and drug him outside and threw him in a snow bank. Fortunately for all of us, after the first shock, he laughed as much as we did. And, since he was laughing, we allowed him to return to his room.

I do remember that...

at NMMI we were the Broncos—our logo was a bucking horse. Our uniform patches had NMMI and the bronco logo. Most of us who had to travel some distance to get to and from home and school traveled in uniform. One reason for the uniform was to attract the attention of young ladies. The standard story was to tell the sweet young thing that we were assigned to the New Mexico Missile Installation and that we employed the Bronco Missile. Sometimes the line worked.

The New Mexico Military Institute

According to the NMMI website, the New Mexico Military Institute, located in Roswell, NM, is the nation's oldest State-supported, nationally accredited, coeducational college preparatory military boarding high school and junior college, offering 4-years of high school and 2 years of college.

For more information about NMMI, visit their website at www.nmmi.edu.

WEST POINT

EXPERIENCES

My military career began the day I raised my hand on the Plain at West Point and was sworn into the US Army.

I was thinking…

of my first, or plebe, year at West Point. My roommate, Bob, wasn't very neat and seemed never to have enough sleep—he could fall asleep pretty-much anytime, anywhere. It turned out that he did have a medical problem, but he didn't get it diagnosed until one day when he fell asleep standing at a blackboard doing a math problem—yeah, during class. The way our math classes ran, the prof would lecture and then tell us to "take boards." The blackboards were sectioned off so each of us had our own space—and we were not to look around; our eyes were to be on our own boards only—unless the prof told us to look elsewhere. Then the prof would give us a problem; we were to solve it as he walked around checking our progress. One day Bob was at the board next to me. After a few minutes of working on a problem I heard a loud CLACK; I couldn't help but look. Bob had dropped his chalk—the clack. He was standing, facing his board, with his nose about ½ inch from the board; he was sound asleep. The prof yelled at him, which woke him up—and shortly thereafter he received medical help and got his issues under control.

I remember that ...

during my plebe year, we had to eat at attention, very stiff and square. There were times when we didn't get a lot to eat. Well, Wednesday night was steak night; it was tradition that the plebes at each dining room table would provide a skit or some entertainment for the upperclassmen, and, as a result, would be allowed to "fall-out," or eat normally.

I don't remember why, but I was in the school's very extensive museum earlier that week and saw a very mean-looking Nazi-made sub-machine gun. Back in those innocent days, I just checked it out. I was going to do a skit with a German accent, and we plebes could enjoy our steaks. Well, I couldn't carry it into the mess hall, as we marched in formally. So I went into the mess hall early and placed the machine-gun on my chair. Well, one of the waiters who was preparing the table for the meal stumbled upon it, freaked out, and someone in authority came and took it. Imagine my surprise when I got there and my machine-gun was gone.

The concern didn't last long as an officer showed up at the table with my weapon wanting to know which dumb plebe had left a machine-gun out where civilian waiters could get to it. I got a good chewing out—but then a good laugh—and certainly did enjoy my steak.

I'll never forget that...

as a plebe playing intramural football on my company's team, I made the last tackle of the last practice play before the season was to start—and tore a ligament in my right knee. I had surgery and stayed in the hospital for several weeks in recovery. Initially, I had to get around in a wheel chair; because my leg was in a cast, I had a board sticking out in front of me on which my casted-leg rested. We referred to such a wheel chair as "modified stock." Being cadets, we had to find things to do in our spare time, and wheel-chair races were a favorite. The problem was that the nurses didn't think that was a good idea and the only straight run was right past their office, so races were typically at night when there might be only one nurse on duty, and we needed good intel on where he/she might be. But we did have races almost every night. Surprisingly, crashes were few. I might add, with appropriate humbleness, that when I left I held the record in the modified-stock category. Ah, youth; it's a shame they waste it on the young.

I was thinking about...

the period after my hospital stay for my football knee; I had been discharged. When I got back to my company, they were just assigning cadets to winter company intramural sports teams. Since I'm 6'3" tall, and had been goofing off at the hospital, they decided I could box heavy weight for the boxing team. To make an understatement, I dislike boxing—but I had no choice. One day I realized that I'd be boxing another plebe who was much bigger and more muscular than I was. To say I was nervous would be an understatement. However, during the first round I noticed that while he threw very powerful blows—he always ducked his head when he punched. I was home free. I was able to avoid many of his punches—I should note that the ones he landed really hurt—and was able to counter punch frequently. I still don't remember which one of us won that fight. I do remember being thankful that I was still alive.

How could I ever forget that...

plebes, as freshmen are known, are, of course the lowest of life forms. Indeed, we were required to memorize that plebes, also called 4th classmen, outrank: "the Superintendent's dog, the Commandant's cat, the Hell Cats (the bandsmen who played reveille for us) the waiters in the mess hall, and all the admirals in the whole damn navy, sir." Well, there were frequent exchange visits between all the academies—and on one occasion there was a senior midshipman (from the US Naval Academy at Annapolis) at our dinner table in the dining hall. Plebes were required to provide services to upper class-men at the table. Well, the midshipman asked for something that I could provide, probably a drink— I delivered it to him, but didn't call him "sir." He complained to the West Point Cadet in charge of the table that I had not rendered him the appropriate military courtesy. I was asked why I had violated military custom. My answer, of course, was that I don't call people "sir" that I outrank. I was yelled at—and then asked why I felt I outranked him. Of course I recited the passage that a Fourth Classman outranks the Superintendent's dog, the Commandant's cat, the Hell Cats, the waiters in the mess hall, and all the admirals in the whole damn navy. "And, sir,"

I said, "I outrank admirals, and I know an admiral outranks him." Everyone but the Middy thought that was wonderful—so I got away with it. Ah, the good old days.

Army-Navy Game

The Army Black Knights of West Point and the Navy Midshipmen of Annapolis have met on the field of battle (football that is) 115 times. They first played in 1890. The Army-Navy rivalry has always been fierce while still remembering both are on the same side when push comes to shove.

As of 2014, the Navy has a 13-game winning streak, but the Colonel thinks this is just a fluke, and a run of bad luck. The Black Knights will soon rise again to re-establish dominance.

I thought it would be a real advantage that…

as a Boy Scout, actually, to be more specific, as an Explorer Scout, I did a lot of rappelling—going down walls and cliffs on ropes. When I arrived at West Point, the summer after our plebe Year they took us to Camp Buckner (a part of the West Point training area) for field training, and one of the first activities was rappelling. It was only a 40 or 50 foot cliff, so it was no big deal. I picked a spot about half way down that I'd bounce off of and then to the ground. (I'd done it hundreds of times before.) So they hooked me up, and I pushed off. Then I discovered that there was a difference; all the work I'd done with scouts was done on hemp rope. I was now on nylon rope—and that rope stretched. My feet hit exactly where I wanted them to, but my body kept moving. I crashed and burned and ended up up-side-down. Not a very impressive first rappel. I was very glad that I hadn't mentioned to anyone that I was experienced at rappelling. I did have to do a lot of push-ups. Ah, the days of my youth.

I was remembering that...

West Point hosted an annual Student Conference on United States Affairs. Students from all over the country came to discuss, in various forums, a number of matters critical to our nation. I always participated as this was good learning and great fun. Oh, and it was an opportunity to meet some young ladies—West Point was all male when I was there. One year in one of the conference groups I was in there was a very, well, nasty—really unfriendly—young lady. I don't remember that she had a nice word to say ever. Most attendees avoided her.

Also at West Point is a wooded trail known as Flirtation Walk. It's a place where a bit more than flirting can take place. And on the trail is a large rock that overhangs the trail; tradition has it that if ever a young lady refuses a kiss while passing under the rock—well, not only will the rock fall, but perhaps all of the walls of all of the buildings at the Point. From personal experience I can vouch for the fact that this tradition has gained many a cadet many a kiss.

Anyway, I decided to invite the unfriendly young lady in my conference group to go for a walk one afternoon; she agreed. As we walked she was quite withdrawn and silent.

Following my plan, I took her on to Flirty, as Flirtation Walk is commonly known. As we approached Kissing Rock I explained the tradition—and waited. She gave me an icy stare—and off we walked. No, I was not broken hearted.

By the way, the rock didn't fall.

The Women of West Point

The first females to join the Corps of Cadets was on July 7, 1976. The first class of women was composed of 119 cadets. Of those 119, 62 women walked across Michie Stadium to graduate in May 1980.

All 62 became Second Lieutenants in the army, thus making military history.

While it's not quite the same now, I was remembering that...

when I was a cadet the Army Football Team was darned good. We played Penn State and Syracuse every year—and usually won.

One year we played Syracuse in NYC's Polo Grounds. We cadets always marched onto the field before the game—then ran into the stands.

One year someone had the idea to have designated cadets carry oranges; when we stopped in the middle of the field for a salute, we'd drop the oranges. Once we were in the stands, everyone could see that they spelled something like "go army" or "beat Syracuse"—I don't remember. On cue, we dropped our oranges. As we ran off the field, more than a few of us stepped on or kicked the dropped oranges.

The message was for the Syracuse fans—so the sports writers, who were behind us, saw that the message was upside down to them—so they ridiculed us for doing it wrong. I mean, why would anyone do anything except for the benefit of the reporters? I think they even printed what they saw (up-side down) in the newspaper.

I also remember some comments from the Syracuse fans who saw us holding the oranges and thought that we were going to throw the oranges at them.

Anyway, we won, 9-2.

Army Black Knights Football

Commonly known as "Army", the Black Knights is the football team representing the United States Military Academy at West Point in New York.

The Black Knights is a three-time national champion (winning in 1944, 1945 and 1946) and is a member of the NCAA Division I Football Bowl Subdivision.

Army football boasts three winners of the Heisman Trophy: Doc Blanchard (1945), Glenn Davis (1946), and Pete Dawkins (1958)

I was thinking about...

the summer I spent in Europe as a West Point cadet. I don't think it still works this way, but way back when (I was a senior there 50 years ago) cadets spent a month assigned to an army unit in Europe as a more-or-less acting 2LT. Cadets did this either the summer before their junior year or the summer before their senior year; I went just before my senior year. Cadets were also authorized 30 days of leave each summer, so many of us took that leave and saw Europe—I did. Three of my classmates and I purchased Eur-rail passes and visited Paris and many other interesting places. In Amsterdam, the Netherlands, we rented a room in an inn and saw the town. There was a very attractive young lady that worked there with whom all of us kidded and flirted.

One evening as we turned in we asked her to be sure we were up at a certain time the next morning as we were taking a tour and couldn't be late.

The next morning, she knocked on the door at the appropriate time; we said that we were awake. About 10 min later she came by the room, listened, heard no activity, so she came in and literally dumped us out of our beds. We were all rather embarrassed as we hit the floor wearing whatever it was we were sleeping in. She left with a very big smirk. We never asked for a wake-up call again.

The Origins of Reveille

Every soldier hears the bugle sounding reveille thousands of times during his or her career. The name comes from réveille (or réveil), the French word for "wake up".

Most US bases play the bugle wake-up call at or near sunrise, and raise the American flag at the same time.

Here's one version of the lyrics:

You've got to get up

You've got to get up

You've got to get up this morning

You've got to get up

You've got to get up

Get up with the bugler's call

The major told the captain

The captain told the sergeant

The sergeant told the bugler

The bugler told them all

My pride won't let me forget that...

   while I was not and am not a great chess player, I did join the Cadet Chess Club. I did learn to improve my game, but I was never a deep-thinking chess player. I was more into action than strategy. It turned out that I was really good at setting up chess matches with other clubs—and that meant trips away from West Point, and such trips were among the most desirable activities for cadets. Hey, we got off post to some civilian area where we slept in hotel rooms and ate good chow, and there were normally some lovely ladies around who were impressed with us. Thus, I found myself elected to be the Captain of the Chess Club. That was necessary because the team we were going to play would tell us how many players they had—and players were ranked; the best played the first board—that's chess board. The second best player played the second board, etc. Since I wasn't a particularly skilled player, the only way we could be sure that I was going on any trip was for me to be captain; and, yes, I always played the last board.

   I remember playing against a club in NYC. We were seven or eight moves into the game and my opponent had taken nearly a half hour to study his next move; then he made it. I made my response in about two minutes. I assumed he'd take another half hour, so I walked around and checked on how the rest of my team was doing; I returned to find my opponent had still not moved. I went and found their team captain and set up a re-match for a couple of months out—and returned just in time to see my opponent move. Again, I responded in about two minutes. Need I say that he beat me? The truth is that I rarely won in such environments. But I sure did enjoy the city and the freedom of being away from West Point.

And, I can honestly tell folks that I was the Captain of the West Point Chess team. Pretty impressive, huh?

Where Did Chess Come from?

Some historians believe chess originated in China, but the majority believe it started in India prior to the 6th century AD. From there it spread to Persia, where it was popularized in the Muslim world. From there it made its way to Southern Europe. During the 15th century in Europe, chess evolved into its current form. The first world chess championship was in 1886. (And no, Denny did not compete that year.)

I was remembering that...

during my Sophomore year, called the Third Class year or Yearling year, my roommate and I lived on the top floor of a five-story barracks. We were studying one Friday evening because we always had Saturday morning classes. For some reason we started feeling, well, a bit mischievous.

We always had big inspections of our rooms on Saturday mornings, so all cadets were both studying and cleaning/polishing. A couple of our classmates had a room directly beneath us, and those guys were the super-shiny, super-sharp kind of cadets. My roomie and I took paper bags, lunch bag size, and filled them with water, stapled them to long strings and swung them out the window—and into the window of the room beneath us. We didn't expect to score a direct hit, but we did. It went right in the window—nothing but net on that shot. We just sat back and waited for revenge. It came.

A few minutes later the folks from downstairs opened our door and slammed it shut on a newspaper—this jammed the door shut—it could only be opened from the outside; we were stuck. Then they poured waste-baskets of water under the door, flooding us. We laughed; we deserved it. We were still discussing how to clean things up when the door burst open and our classmates from down stairs ran in and started cleaning out the water.

It seems that the floor leaked—and it was raining in their very, very neat and clean room. We laughed and sat and watched them clean up our room. There were certain advantages to living on the top floor.

About the US Military Academy

The idea of forming a national military academy was first conceived by President George Washington. Then Secretary of State, Thomas Jefferson, argued against the idea stating there was no provision for it in the constitution. Also, many in congress saw the idea as too aristocratic to pursue.

Despite his early opposition, on 16 March 1802 President Jefferson signed legislation that formally created the Corps of Engineers" which "shall be stationed at West Point and constitute a Military Academy.

And thus began the long and noble tradition of West Point.

I was thinking about...

a goofy day at West Point; the following day my regiment was to bus to New York City to march in a parade; that afternoon we were called to a company formation for an unknown reason. Suddenly, a bunch of buses pulled up near us, and the thousand or so cadets who were going to the parade were told to (they really, truly said this) practice loading the buses. Well, being good soldiers who had little choice in the matter, we did as we were told and, over the next half hour or so, we boarded the buses a number of times. Yes, the next day, in full parade uniform, we boarded them again, like a bunch of good little cadets, and we did it so well—after all, we had practiced. I did learn a big lesson from this: never would I tolerate doing such a stupid thing as making my troops practice loading a bus, and I never did. That practice loading buses was perhaps the stupidest thing I ever did at the Point.

I was thinking…

that, as far as I know, I still hold two records at West Point. The first I set as a plebe. I am the only cadet in the history of the Point to be ordered not to sing, even at football rallies ("Just mouth the words, Mr. Gillem," I was ordered by the senior cadets in front of me.) Now, I think I have a great voice; I know all the words to the songs I enjoy, and I like to sing. That said, my wife and I were attending a small church once; the choir was directly in front of and facing the congregation. We took a seat in the front row. After the service the choir leader asked me, nicely, if I would sit somewhere else in the future. Apparently I'd made a major impact on the choir.

My second record involved a major paper I had to submit during my senior year. In that paper I spelled the word "maintenance" seven different ways, none of them correctly. My professor told me that was a record. And now, thanks to spell-check (we had typewriters) my record is safe.

In a funny coincidence…

last week I visited my dentist, and that visit reminded me of the money I made as a brand new Second Lieutenant (2LT) over 50 years ago. I don't currently have dental insurance, so it's pay-as-you-go; I hadn't paid for a previous visit, so when I paid when I left; the bill was $222.30. You see, in June of 1964 the base pay of a new 2LT was $222.30. We were also paid $47.88 as subsistence allowance (for food) unless we were eating in a mess hall. As a cadet at West Point, our pay was half that of a 2LT, so we made $111.15 per month. From this vast sum we purchased our books, uniforms, and personal items—even had a few bucks for weekends. Indeed, as was the custom back then, during senior year, we all purchased new cars. We were permitted to take possession of them and have them on post starting in April. Our pay was enough to cover all of this. I bought a new Oldsmobile—and paid it off during my first Vietnam tour in 65-66. This thinking of my Army pay reminded me that during my second tour in Vietnam in 67-68 I was a captain drawing jump pay, family separation allowance, combat pay, virtually every kind of specialty pay there was; in June I went over four-years of service for pay, and I was making a bit over $1000 a month; wasn't sure what

I'd do with all that money. Fortunately, I had a wife at home helping me with that problem. Anyway, the lowest private today probably makes ten times what I did as a new shave-tail. Ah, the good old days – when gas was about 20 cents a gallon.

What is a Shavetail?

According to dictionary.com, an army shavetail is defined as:

Word Origin: noun, slang.

1. U.S. Army. a second lieutenant.

2. a young, newly broken mule.

The term originated circa 1840-50, in reference to unbroken army mules, whose tails were shaved for identification.

FORT BENNING

*After graduation from USMA we all spent
2 months on graduation leave before
beginning out training. For most of us that
was Fort Benning, GA—Benning School
for Boys. I went to Airborne School first
(learning how to jump out of perfectly good
aircraft while in flight), then pulled some
extra duty while waiting to begin Ranger
School. I graduated as a Ranger in mid-
December 1964. Back then, Benning
was the Infantry School and the home of
Airborne and Ranger Schools. Now it's
much more; the Armor School is there, too,
and a lot more women are involved as cadre
as well as being trained.*

I was thinking about...

my first jump out of an aircraft in flight. I'm afraid of heights—so, to help get control of this fear I volunteered for both Airborne and Ranger schools when I graduated from West Point.

I arrived at Fort Benning, GA, in August of 1964 and signed in to Airborne school. The three-week training began a few days later. The hundred or so troops in my class were divided, first into platoons of about 40 men. These were then divided into groups of ten called "sticks." As it turns out, a stick is composed of all the paratroopers who are going to jump out of a given door of an airplane. For whatever reason, since half the class were new second lieutenants, I was made the leader of my stick.

During the first two weeks of training, I had little to do as a stick leader except to make sure all my troops were in formation, and they always were. The third week was jump week. The C-123 aircraft we would jump from had two jump doors—one on each side of the aircraft. One stick would jump from each of them. As we approached the drop zone we got a series of commands: Stand Up (we were riding sitting down wearing our parachutes); Hook Up (our chutes would be opened by a static line that would pull them open once we were far enough away from the aircraft—and we had to hook to the cable in the plane) Check Equipment (we checked to make sure our parachute was still on properly; the person behind us checked the back of the chute); Sound Off For Equipment Check, and, finally, Stand In The Door (the stick leader would move to the door and get ready to jump; the rest of the stick would be right behind him). So, who was the first one in the door; yes, me, the guy who was afraid of heights.

I had to stand in the open door with one hand on the outside of each side of the door, with half of my lead foot outside the aircraft, in a crouch, and wait for the command to Jump, which would be accompanied by a slap on my butt. I was going to be in the door like that for several minutes. I remember well; I was just plain scared. I started telling myself it was okay—I was wearing a parachute and was planning to jump out—so falling was no big deal. After a minute or so I started relaxing a bit and enjoying the view. Then I noticed someone falling under the airplane; that was weird. Then, I noticed that it was the guy who was the stick leader for the stick on the other side of my aircraft. I wondered why he'd been told to jump and I hadn't. I turned around to ask… and it was obvious. The Jumpmaster had said jump and slapped me about 4 times—I was frozen in the door. So, I turned around and jumped. It was a great feeling. AIRBORNE!

As a brand new 2nd lieutenant…

I had just graduated from Airborne School and was awaiting Ranger School—so for about a month I was available to do any odd tasks around Fort Benning. One of my tasks was to run a live-fire exercise demonstration. A platoon was going to attack a hill. We used live ammunition to fire into the hill as preparatory fire before the platoon attacked. The platoon would also fire live ammo. But the machine-guns that were supporting the attack would switch to blank rounds as the platoon moved towards the objective, because we wanted no chance of live rounds hitting the soldiers. I had the machine-gunners briefed and had boxes of both live and blank rounds next to their guns. As the exercise began, my machine-guns were, properly firing live rounds. Then, as the troops started moving, I commanded "Switch to blank." This was how we had rehearsed things. As I was walking among the machine-gunners I became aware that one was still firing live ammo. I grabbed him, pulled him away from his gun and started chewing. His response: Sir, when you called "Switch to blank," I though you said to "wave at the bank." So I did. Fortunately, no one was hurt that day, but that young soldier's pride was severely damaged by the time I was done with him. Then his sergeant took over.

As a new 2nd lieutenant...

I'd just graduated from Airborne School and was awaiting Ranger School. I had the opportunity to observe a demonstration of some new equipment. In this case the new Armored Personnel Carrier (APC) was being demonstrated to some visiting senior officers from Australia. The demonstration, at a local small lake, showed their ability to swim. When the demonstration was over the officer in charge decided it would be a good idea to offer a ride to the visiting VIPs. Of course, there was an extra APC on site; it was there just in case something went wrong with one of the others. Someone found the driver and cranked up the vehicle. They put the VIPs in the back and headed for the lake. A few yards out into the lake the APC sank; at first all we could see was Australian bush-hats floating on the water. All the people were safe. It seems that the driver, not expecting to be used, never got around to ensuring that the belly plate on the APC was soundly seated; it wasn't. I have to admit that I thought it was very funny, but I was just an observer.

I can still remember the aches that came from this…

While current standards require all who would attend Ranger School be parachute qualified before attending; that wasn't true back then. That said, I had just graduated from Airborne School and was proud of not being a "dirty leg" any more. Because the proper technique to land in a parachute involves having one's legs bent as you touch the ground, non-paratroopers are pejoratively called Straight-Legs or just Legs or, sometimes, Dirty Legs. Oh, and ranger students wear no rank—we're all just rangers.

As new ranger students we spent a lot of time in the hand-to-hand combat pit. This was a very large saw-dust filled pit where we learned and practiced hits, throws, and the like. It was interesting, if dirty and tiring, and it seemed to go on forever. One day I was fighting one of my fellow ranger buddies when one of the instructors came over to coach and harass us. When I looked at the instructor (he expected me to attack him, that was the drill) I noticed that he was a sergeant and had not yet been to airborne school; I did know that he was going there shortly. Anyway, as I moved toward him I called him a Dirty Leg. I knew the minute I did it that it was a mistake, but the words were already out of my mouth. My words did what I expected; they embarrassed and angered him. And, no surprise, he took it out on me. I may have been better at parachuting than he was at the moment, but he was much better at hand-to-hand combat than I was. I went back to the barracks quite sore from that time in the hand-to-hand pit. But I was rather proud of myself.

The Army Ranger Motto

The Army Ranger motto was first coined on 6 June 1944, during the assault on Dog White sector of Omaha Beach as part of the invasion of Normandy. Brigadier General Norman Cota (assistant CO of the 29th ID) asked Major Max Schneider, CO of the 5th Ranger Battalion "What outfit is this?", Schneider answered "5th Rangers, Sir!" To this, Cota replied "Well, goddamnit, if you're Rangers, lead the way!" From this, the Ranger motto—"Rangers lead the way!"—was born

I was thinking about…

Ranger School consisted of three 3-week phases. One of the big things about the final three weeks of Ranger School, which was held in the swamps around Eglin Air Force Base in Florida, was the alligators. It was traditional for each group of rangers to have their picture taken with a gator. Of course, there was an old female, one-eyed gator that was tame enough to be used for all these pictures. Yes, I have such a picture.

It seems that a few years after I was there, Old One Eye needed surgery to remove a growth on one of her legs. Here's the story: The Eglin AFB vet couldn't get the proper anesthesia, but he said cold would put her to sleep. There was a nearby Air Base with big environmental hanger that had a sub-zero testing room. On the day of the operation, the Ranger sergeant in charge of the alligators tied up Old One Eye using proper Ranger knots (a key point). An Air Force helicopter flew her up to the environmental hanger and she was taken into the cold room. As the temperature was lowered, she got lethargic and finally seemed to be in hibernation. The operation was a success, and the patient was trussed up, but not by Ranger qualified individuals.

On the flight back to the Ranger Camp, Old One Eye

revived and became active. She started moving vigorously, slipped out of the ropes holding her immobile, and started to thrash around in the back of the chopper. It was reported that both crew chiefs were screaming. The helicopter made a very fast landing on the helo pad at the Ranger Camp; they opened the door and Old One Eye slid out onto the concrete. The helicopter immediately took off. It took several sergeants to get her under control and back into her pen. She survived her ordeal and her leg healed fine. Isn't that a very happy ending?

Army Ranger Training Begins

On September 1950 at Fort Benning Georgia Ranger Training began with the formation of 17 Airborne Companies by the Ranger Training Command. The first Ranger class graduated in November 1950." The United States Army's Infantry School officially created the Ranger Department in December 1951. The first Ranger School Class was conducted in January–March 1952. Its duration was 59 days. Ranger training was voluntary at the time.

I graduated from Ranger School in December—and I remembered a story one of my West Point classmates, Bill, told me…

When Bill graduated he went into the Air Force. After returning from tours in South East Asia, Bill was assigned to the Air Force Special Operations Wing at Hurlburt Field. Hulburt was near the Army's Florida Ranger Camp—where ranger trainees went through the swamp phase of Ranger School. One of Bill's tasks was to talk with Ranger classes about Air-Ground Operations, the limitations, the capabilities, and the need for good team work. On several occasions he was invited by the cadre to go out and observe the guys slogging through the swamp. In his opinion, and mine, too, the worst time was in the winter. The troops were cold, tired, and miserable.

Since all of the guys in my West Point class who went Army (most of us) were required to go to Ranger School, Bill got an appreciation for a small part of what we all went through.

For some reason the Ranger cadre liked Bill (he was a Dirty Leg), and he was invited to attend a formal graduation party (Dining In) at the Hurlburt Officers Club. Everyone assembled in formal mess dress uniforms. The dinner bell was rung and then a young lieutenant stood up and requested permission for those assembled to pass all the silverware to the head table. This was not a normal part of a formal dining in, but isn't unusual for Rangers to do. This was done and everyone sat down eating with their fingers; these are Rangers, remember. Bill glanced up and saw an Air Force officer enter the room. He was informed this was a private party and asked politely to leave. He was full of himself and announced. "I am an Air Force Officer; this is my club, and I can go anywhere I please." The Rangers nodded and beckoned for him to come in further. They then set upon him, stripped him buck naked, and tore all his clothes into small bits. Bill said the last he saw of him was as he exited red faced, crying, and clad only in a table cloth to the accompaniment of many loud Hurrahs. Some people need to learn the hard way. For Bill it was NEVER MESS WITH RANGERS! Amen, Bill, amen.

The Ranger Creed

Recognizing that I volunteered as a Ranger, fully knowing the hazards of my chosen profession, I will always endeavor to uphold the prestige, honor, and high esprit de corps of my Ranger Regiment.

Acknowledging the fact that a Ranger is a more elite soldier who arrives at the cutting edge of battle by land, sea, or air, I accept the fact that as a Ranger my country expects me to move further, faster, and fight harder than any other soldier.

Never shall I fail my comrades. I will always keep myself mentally alert, physically strong, and morally straight and I will shoulder more than my share of the task whatever it may be, one hundred percent and then some.

Gallantly will I show the world that I am a specially selected and well trained soldier. My courtesy to superior officers, neatness of dress, and care of equipment shall set the example for others to follow.

Energetically will I meet the enemies of my country. I shall defeat them on the field of battle for I am better trained and will fight with all my might. Surrender is not a Ranger word. I will never leave a fallen comrade to fall into the hands of the enemy and under no circumstances will I ever embarrass my country.

Readily will I display the intestinal fortitude required to fight on to the Ranger objective and complete the mission, though I be the lone survivor.
Rangers, lead the way!

COMPANY GRADE OFFICER (2ND LIEUTENANT, 1ST LIEUTENANT, AND CAPTAIN)

As a general rule in the army, companies are commanded by captains and assisted by lieutenants. Thus, these ranks are called Company Grade officers. Majors, Lieutenant Colonels, and Colonels are called Field Grade Officers. Above them are General Officers.

In early January 1965 I reported to Fort Carson, CO, where I was assigned as a rifle platoon leader in the 2nd Battalion, 11th Infantry. Sometime in May I volunteered for service in Vietnam—I think I was afraid the war would end before I was able to get to it. My request was denied, because, at the time, we had only advisors in Vietnam, and, quite reasonably, no one wanted a second lieutenant as an advisor. Apparently, the day after my denial was mailed to me, our Army started landing combat units in Vietnam, because I had orders for Vietnam before mid-June. I departed for Vietnam that October.

I was thinking about…

one of the goofiest things that happened to me as a second lieutenant. I was living in Bachelor Officers Quarters, or BOQ, at Fort Carson, CO. The BOQs were a series of one-bedroom apartments down a hall, with a large common area at the end. I went off on a couple of weeks of temporary duty. When I returned one evening I went to my BOQ and my room was gone—gone! The common area had been expanded and my room was gone. Fortunately my platoon sergeant lived in the barracks with our troops; I knocked on his door and ended up sleeping on an air mattress on his floor. The next day I was told that when the remodeler arrived to work on my old BOQ room they looked for me. When they couldn't find me they told my company, and a bunch of my troops moved my stuff to a room in the next BOQ; they'd set everything up just as I'd had it. Well, guess what. My new BOQ was the next one to be remodeled; the workers had a key, entered my new room, took all my things, which had been hung in the closet or placed in drawers, and threw them on the bed and tossed a sheet over everything and did their painting and repairs. They then left the room—wide open. To make an understatement, everything was a mess, some things were damaged, and some missing. I did finally get everything resolved, but what a pain all that was. On the other hand, the guy living in the next BOQ room, my new neighbor, was the guy who later introduced me to the lady who became my wife. That was a good move for a lucky guy.

Fort Carson Colorado

In 1954 Camp Carson was redesignated as Fort Carson. In the 1960s, mechanized units were assigned to the fort and it was expanded to the present 137,000 acres. Between 1963 and 1966 Butts Army Air Field was constructed with a 4,573-foot runway for light fixed-wing aircraft.

Throughout its history Fort Carson has been home to nine divisions. Presently, the following units are based there:

4th Infantry Division, 10th Special Forces Group, 440th Civil Affairs Battalion, 71st Ordnance Group, 4th Engineer Battalion, 1st Battalion, 25th Aviation Regiment, 759th Military Police Battalion, 10th Combat Support Hospital, 43rd Sustainment Brigade, Army Field Support Battalion-Fort Carson, 423rd Transportation Company (USAR) and the 13th Air Support Operations Squadron

I was thinking about…

my first troop assignment at Fort Carson, CO. I served as a rifle platoon leader in a mechanized rifle company for about six months followed by an assignment to battalion headquarters for just over a month. For what turned out to be my final assignment at Fort Carson, I was made the executive officer (XO), or second in command, of one of the rifle companies. The Commanding Officer of this company was an old soldier. Captain (CPT) Conway had been a sergeant before being commissioned as an officer, and he was a senior captain at the time. He really knew the army. As long as you were on his good side, not an easy place to stay, he was a great guy to watch and learn from. He was very good at, well, "B-S"ing people. One time I saw him walk a couple of senior officers through the company barracks at a time when we were not ready for inspection; I don't remember why. The captain was directing the visitors' eyes from this rifle to that locker to some other item; basically he was showing them the few items that were really squared away. They were literally stepping over junk, but they never seemed to notice it as the boss danced them through the company—it was an art-form. CPT Conway left the company shortly after I joined, but I never forgot watching him in action. I learned from him. He was a real educator.

Vietnam

*I flew to Vietnam on a chartered airliner
full of army guys going to war. When I got
there I reported to the replacement center
and was subsequently assigned as a rifle
platoon leader in Company B, 1st Battalion,
18th Infantry, 1st Infantry Division (The Big
Red One).*

I was thinking about...

my first shower in Vietnam. I had joined my rifle platoon during an operation. We would be returning to our camp in two days. I suggested that the platoon sergeant who'd been running the platoon keep running it, while I watched him. That was a good move. Nevertheless, I was very busy, learning the platoon members, learning the terrain, learning about the enemy, and moving through the jungle tactically. When we got back to our tent-city we were all dirty—and it was raining. Thinking there were probably no showers anywhere around, I stripped and went out into the rain. I got wet and soaped up and...the rain stopped. So, I went, naked from tent to tent and leaned against each tent; this caused the water had not yet run off the tent tops to pour down on me. It worked, but I am sure I looked like a jerk, and I never tried that stunt again.

I was thinking about…

my first tour in Vietnam in 1966. Our battalion had been assigned an area where we were to move in and build a base camp. Almost all the structures were tents, and it was decided that the mess hall should be on a concrete slab. Someone noticed that I was a West Point grad; back in those days all West Pointers majored in engineering; we had only four electives during our entire four years. Anyway, I was told to survey a spot for the mess hall's concrete slab. I obtained some survey gear from some artillery folks and laid out a nice rectangular place for the slab and had my little team mark the corners with stakes in the ground. We then turned in all the surveying gear, and, as I was walking back to my tent, I realized that I'd done nothing to indicate how to make the slab level. I was glad that I'd realized that, so I reassembled my little team, checked out the survey gear again, and had marks made on each stake how high up the stake the concrete had to go for the slab to be level.

The moral of this story is that an engineering degree does not an engineer make. But, it all worked, and I only got kidded a little bit.

I was thinking about…

a time in Vietnam when I was a rifle platoon leader. My platoon, as a part of my company and battalion, was about to conduct a frontal attack on a very probable enemy position. We would be attacking over about 100 meters of open rice-patty. There was a big tree right in the middle of the patty; other than that it was all wide open, right up to the tree line where we thought the enemy was located. We were quite sure that the enemy didn't know we were there. Just before it was time to attack I was assigned a news reporter and camera-man to go with me. I told them to stay behind my troops and not to bother them in any way as we were about to attack and disruption could cause death. As I went to check the troops one more time I saw the reporter and camera man jogging out to the tree in front of us—so they could photograph us as we began the attack. They clearly gave away our position to the enemy. I think I would have shot them, but one of my great sergeants grabbed me. We made the attack; it turned out that when the enemy realized we were there they pulled out. The reporter made it clear that he was only concerned with getting a good story and pictures that would make him look good to his editor. It was equally clear that he cared not a bit that all of my men could have been killed or wounded because of his action; he really didn't care. I later met other (not all) media folks who seemed to have the same attitude. Maybe that's why I have zero respect for some of our nation's Main Stream Media.

French Indochina

In the late 1850s, France began its conquest of Indochina and completed it by 1893. The 1884 Treaty of Huế formed the basis for French colonial rule in Vietnam for the next 70 years. Despite military resistance, primarily from the Cần Vương of Phan Đình Phùng, by 1888 the area of the current-day nations of Cambodia and Vietnam was made into the colony of French Indochina.

I was thinking about...

the first time that I was ever shot at—in combat, of course. It was on my first tour in Vietnam as a rifle platoon leader in the 1st Infantry Division, the Big Red One. My company was moving through some thick jungle looking for an enemy base-camp. My platoon was leading the company, and we weren't finding anything. The Company Commander (CO) called for a halt and for all platoon leaders (the company had three rifle platoons) to join him. My troops got down, established some good firing positions, and started probing out to our front, exactly what they were supposed to be doing. I was talking with the CO and the other officers when there was a huge, nearby boom and bullets were flying everywhere. We all hit the ground. Needless to say, I was afraid. The obvious thing for all of us to do was to get back to our platoons quickly. I decided to get up and run back to the platoon, but after I got up on my knees and got my right foot out in front of me I just couldn't get my left leg and foot to move so I could stand up. This was likely a response to the fear that was running through me—along with adrenalin. So, I ran on one foot and one knee; that was the best I could do. After a dozen or so steps my left foot decided to cooperate, and I went the rest of the way on two feet. I'll bet I was one funny looking second lieutenant as I began my run, but no one was laughing.

It turns out that when the CO told us to stop, my platoon was just a few yards from the enemy base camp we were looking for, and the probing my guys were doing found them. They were as surprised as we were, and there were a lot more of them than we expected. My platoon kept them engaged and covered the rest of the company while they moved away; then we fell back under fire. Then we worked the area over with artillery and air strikes. I'm glad we didn't have smart-phones back then; someone would have filmed me waddling back to my platoon.

The Claymore Mine

The M18A1 Claymore, first used in Vietnam in 1966, is a directional anti-personnel mine. Its inventor, Norman MacLeod, named the mine after a large Scottish medieval sword. The Claymore is command-detonated and directional, meaning it is fired by remote-control and shoots a pattern of metal balls into the kill zone like a shotgun.

Maximum range is 110 yd within a 60° arc in front of the device. It is used primarily in ambushes and as an anti-infiltration device against enemy infantry.

THE GENERAL'S AIDE

*After serving as a platoon leader for six
months I was interviewed by a newly
promoted brigadier general who was just
assigned as an assistant division commander
of my division. Brigadier General
Hollingsworth hired me on the spot—despite
the fact that I was taller than he was and
had little understanding about how senior
headquarters worked; I guess he liked me.
This job was quite an education for me.*

I was thinking about...

the last half of my first tour in Vietnam. I was an aide to an assistant division commander, a one-star or brigadier general. After he hired me, the general went off for a couple of days of briefings at our higher headquarters. I had two junior enlisted men to assist me in taking care of the general, an orderly and a driver. While the general was gone we got his quarters squared away. The one thing missing was a military wrist watch. I went to the Division Headquarters Company supply room to get a watch. The supply sergeant had a new one put aside for the new general. I opened the box and wound the watch and was going to set the time on it—when the stem came off in my hand. I gave it back to the supply sergeant and told him I needed another one for the general; the supply sergeant didn't have another one.

I was in my office pondering what to do when the Division Sergeant Major walked through. He saw my frown and asked about my problem. When I explained my situation, he said he could help if we could use my jeep. We then drove a mile or so to the headquarters of the Division's Support Command; this was one of the five major sub-units of the division. We walked in and the Sergeant Major chatted with people. We ended up in the office of the Support Command Sergeant Major. After we had chatted for a while the Support Command Sergeant Major asked what he could do for us. At that the Division Command Sergeant Major asked him to stick out his left arm. The division Sergeant Major then removed his wrist watch and gave it to me with the comment, "Lieutenant, if that isn't the best wrist watch in the whole division, this guy should be relieved." And we walked out. God bless Sergeants Major.

Command Sergeant Major

The first official U.S. use of the term was in 1776, when a sergeant major was appointed to the headquarters of each infantry battalion of the Continental Army.

Sergeant Major refers to both a military rank and a specific leadership position. It is the highest enlisted rank, just above first sergeant and master sergeant, with a pay grade of E-9.

Command Sergeant Major is the senior enlisted advisor to the commanding officer of a particular unit.

I was thinking about…

the one time in my life, it was in Vietnam, that I was ordered to sing—and I loved it! You may or may not know that I hold two records at West Point; one of them is that I'm the only cadet in the history of the Corps to be ordered not to sing, even at football rallies ("Just mouth the words, Mr. Gillem," I was ordered by the senior cadets in front of me.) I was an aide to a brigadier general in the First Infantry Division. The division's generals had their own mess, a place to eat and relax. Most of the division staff's senior officers were welcome there, as were we aides. On one occasion a small combo from the division band had been providing some entertainment. As the night wore on, several of us who had consumed a few adult beverages, were singing along with the piano player. He was playing some "oldies." I knew all the words and was having a good time singing. Then a colonel, who was singing with us, turned to me and said, "Lieutenant, you have a horrible voice; shut up." So, shut up I did. It turns out, I was the only one who knew the words, so everyone was just sort-of humming along with the piano. After a couple of minutes the colonel faced me and said, "Sing, lieutenant." I did and thoroughly enjoyed my one and only command performance.

I was thinking about...

my assignment as an aide to an assistant division commander, a brigadier general. My general had just been promoted and was very, very aggressive. We were in our helicopter flying near the border between Vietnam and Cambodia. At this point the border was a rather wide river. The General told the pilots to fly down the river. After a number of miles there started to be trees on both sides of the river and eventually they were tall enough that the branches reached across the river forming a tunnel. The boss said to keep flying into the tunnel. Then we started taking gunfire from both sides of the river. There were two pilots on board, a door-gunner on each side, the General and me. I shot out one door, and the General shot out the other door; we both had M-16 rifles. It seemed like this fight went on for two hours, but I think five minutes was more like it. All I did was shoot and reload, shoot and reload; what other choice did I have? The door gunners fired up all their machine-gun ammunition. The pilots kept the plane in the air and got us up once the tree canopy permitted it. That was one scary ride; I'm not sure how we survived, none of us were wounded, but the chopper had a whole bunch of new holes. Of course, I am sure the enemy wasn't expecting a US helicopter to fly down their river. We all got decorated for that fight, and it sure was an adrenalin rush.

I was thinking about…

my term as an aide-de-camp in Vietnam. Apparently the General wanted an aide with a lot of experience on the ground as a rifle platoon leader. I was introduced to him and hired on the spot. For the first month or so after every tactical briefing we attended, he'd sit me down in his tent, and we would critique the plan from my perspective. This was rather heady stuff for this young lieutenant, but it really made sense because most of the staff had never been out in the woods. One evening we attended a big briefing for a major operation that would kick off the next day. The General asked me about the plan. I responded that it was clear to me than none of the staff had ever been in the jungle. The general responded that he agreed and that was why he made the statements that he did. Then I stuck my neck way out; I said, "Sir, it was clear to me that you had never been in the jungle."

Well… the next day the General ditched me and got himself inserted into the jungle where he spent a day or so with a rifle company. When he came back we had no more critiques, and I got my butt chewed regularly.

All things considered, I'm glad I said what I did, but I sure paid for it.

I was thinking about...

the time in Vietnam when I was an aide to a general. We were in our chopper going somewhere. While in flight my main job was to monitor all the radio frequencies to be sure we knew what was going on. We often worked with the infantry battalion that Australia had deployed to help us. I liked listening to the Australian accents, so I always kept one radio on their frequency. On one occasion, I was so enjoying their chatter that I not only did not monitor the other frequencies, but I also didn't hear the General when he asked me a question. Well, the General smacked my knee; that got me back to the real world. I quickly got caught up on the activities of our units—and didn't have to learn that lesson again.

I was thinking about...

another time as an aide in Vietnam. Most of our days began as we jumped in our helicopter and went off to observe or spend time with the thousands of soldiers who were a part of the First Infantry Division. As my time to rotate home drew near the boss told me to find a replacement. So, I went looking. I found a great lieutenant, who I thought would do a fine job, and the general agreed. My next task was to train him in the job. For a couple of weeks we went everywhere together, with him taking more and more of the responsibility for taking care of the General. Finally, it was clear that I was just getting in the way, and the boss told me I could stay back the next day. The General was very aggressive and, at his direction, we flew in some very dangerous places and often took fire. On my first day not flying with the General a bullet went through the seat I would have been sitting in, had I gone along that day. I felt funny not going out with the team, but I'm glad I didn't go that day.

I was thinking about…

the end of my first tour in Vietnam. I was assigned as an aide to a general, but I had found and broken in my replacement and still had a couple of weeks left in country. Our division headquarters was only 30 or so miles from Saigon, and our general-officers' mess did not have any foreign beers, and our three generals wanted foreign beer. It seems that the longshoremen's unions in the states wouldn't load anything made by non-union workers on a ship bound for Vietnam, and foreign beer fell into that category. My mission was to solve the problem.

I started by calling on the Dutch Ambassador to Vietnam. He said he got Heinekens Beer from the American embassy; he didn't know where they got it. Well, the American embassy would not work with our military on things like supplies, because they brought in stuff involved in diplomacy, you see. Well, I went everywhere and found nothing. Finally, I found a guy who was a smuggler. He flew two planes a week in from Formosa and had connections to avoid customs. He was willing to give me one seat a week just to have the connection with our military. I was about ready to take it, after briefing the General. Then I heard of a club that was run jointly by the embassy and our military. I went there and found that with just a bit of name-dropping I was able to buy all the foreign beer I needed for the good generals.

So, I ended my first tour in Vietnam with a "mission accomplished" hand-shake from my General—and I did it without needing to get into smuggling. Pretty cool, huh?

The Huey Helicopter

The Bell UH-1 helicopter is powered by a single turboshaft engine, with two-bladed main and tail rotors. Over 16,000 have been produced, 7,000 of which saw service in the Vietnam War.

The U.S. Army was the first to use the Huey in combat during the Vietnam War. The original designation of HU-1 led to the helicopter's nickname of Huey. In September 1962, the designation was changed to UH-1, but the nickname "Huey" stuck, and many a grunt owes his life to the beloved aircraft.

MY 1ST RIFLE COMPANY

I left Vietnam and returned to California to spend time with my family—then on to Ohio where a beautiful young lady had been planning our wedding for months. While visiting her and before our wedding, orders arrived assigning me to the 101st Airborne Division at Fort Campbell, KY. While there I was blessed to be given the best job in the Army—command of a rifle company.

I was thinking about...

getting married. I returned safely from my first tour in Vietnam in late Oct 1966. Marilyn and I had gotten engaged just before I deployed; we planned to get married once I returned. We were married on the day after Thanksgiving. My biggest problem, besides putting up with all the girly-girl stuff women go through regarding weddings, was that I was going to wear my dress blue uniform. I had second lieutenant shoulder boards, but was now an exalted first lieutenant, and I was just couple of months away from making Captain. So how was I to get first lieutenant boards when I was in Cleveland, Ohio? Need I say that there are no military clothing sales stores around there? Further, why would I want to buy something that I'd only wear once? Then a classmate suggested that I use white paint and a toothpick to paint the gold second lieutenant bars white (first lieutenants wear silver bars); I did and it worked perfectly.

After our wedding and reception we flew to Philadelphia to attend the Army-Navy game the next day. We stayed at the Ben Franklin Hotel, where we always stayed as cadets. That was fun. The next day, sitting with my new bride, I saw Army beat Navy for the first time. We had lost every year I was a cadet. We did actually win the season after I graduated, but I was in Ranger School at the time and was only able to see some of the game on TV. So, it was a great game. From there we flew to Washington DC where we went to plays, toured the Smithsonian, etc. Our last stop was two days at West Point; it was my wife's first visit to my Rock-bound Highland Home. We returned to Cleveland, Ohio, to pack up our wedding gifts, and off we went to Fort Campbell, KY, where I would assume command an airborne rifle company.

My New Wife

Marilyn grew up in Cleveland, Ohio, where her dad was a high school basketball and football coach. She's the oldest of 5 siblings. She grew up on the sidelines of athletic events, and she knows a great deal more about sports than I do. She remembers that the ride home after the game was either a lot of fun or very, very quiet, depending on whether dad's team won or not. (He won many more times than he lost.) Marilyn was an active swimmer as she grew up, and attended Kent State U where where she majored in Phys Ed and was involved in synchronized swimming. She was employed as a PE teacher at a high school in Cleveland when she met me.

I was thinking about...

Thanksgiving 48 years ago and getting married. As I said, we were to be married the day after Thanksgiving. This meant that the rehearsal dinner was on Thanksgiving Day. Now, I love turkey. I love it hot; I love it cold, but... I have to have it with cranberry sauce; that's not negotiable.

Of course they served us a turkey dinner at our rehearsal dinner. Marilyn and I were, naturally, at the head table with our parents. And, RED ALERT, they didn't serve cranberry sauce with the meal. Because I was more or less blocked in at the head table, I couldn't get up to go find a waiter. While the waiters were always around, I could never get their attention. I was so frustrated that I nearly called the whole marriage thing off, right there.

I confess I'm glad I didn't.

I was thinking about...

when I was first married. After our honeymoon, we headed for Fort Campbell, KY. On-post housing wasn't immediately available, so we rented an apartment in Clarksville, TN, and settled into our first home together. Monday morning I was up early, dressed in my fatigues, ate my usual breakfast of cold cereal and orange juice, and got ready for work. My new bride was up with me, though I wasn't sure why she was up so early, and off I went to work. The next day began the same way. On the third morning I asked her why she didn't just stay in bed. She said something about wanting to make my breakfast. I suggested that I could and did pour my own cereal. She got the message. I never saw her up that early again unless she had somewhere to go. Smart lady.

I was thinking about...

January 1967—in the previous two months, I'd returned from my first tour in Vietnam, was married to my wonderful wife, had reported to Fort Campbell, KY, and the 101st Airborne Division, was assigned to a rifle company. Then, on January 3rd I was promoted to Captain and assumed command of that company. The company first sergeant was sick, thus not around for my first two weeks of command. Then he reported for duty, fit and ready to rock. I am, if you didn't know, a white guy; First Sergeant (1SG) Robert Cook was a black guy. One of the things that was a really big deal in those days was very short haircuts, typically called 'white sidewalls,' which Top (nickname for first sergeant) and I discussed at our first meeting. When he stood in front of the company for the first time since returning from sick-status, he made an announcement I'll never forget. He announced that after a meeting with me the company's troopers now had two choices for haircuts. He went on to say that troopers could get a white-sidewall, if they looked like the captain, or they could get a black-sidewall if they looked like him. Then he asked for questions; there weren't any. Besides being a great 1SG, he also had a great sense of humor.

I was thinking about...

back when I was a company commander in the 101st Airborne Division. I had a great first lieutenant as my executive officer named Mike. He and his wife lived in a nearby mobile home park and were expecting their first child. Two of our second lieutenant platoon leaders also lived in that park and the two bachelors often ate with Mike and his wife. On one occasion the bachelors had shown up for dinner, but had to wait because Mike was not home yet. When he arrived they kidded him about being late. He explained that he'd been out looking for an apartment; they wanted to know why. He pointed out that, if the guys hadn't noticed, they were expecting a baby pretty soon, and would need more room. One of the guys said, "Mike, I don't get it; babies aren't very big. Why do you need more room?" Mike didn't tell me what he said to them in response.

The rest of the story is that those two bachelor lieutenants did deploy to Vietnam later. When they returned both asked the army to send them to medical school, and the army did send both of them. Both of them had full careers as Army physicians. One ended up as Surgeon General of the Army. I suspect that at some point both figured out why it takes more room to have a baby.

I was thinking about…

the only time I saw a colonel chew out a general, a rare sight, indeed. Best of all, he got away with it.

I was a rifle company commander in the 101st Airborne Division, and our companies rotated the duty of being the division's and nation's IRF or Immediate Reaction Force. When the IRF was alerted we had one hour to be fully equipped for combat and at the airfield, ready to draw parachutes and go wherever we were sent. And this particular week, my company was the IRF, and we were called out in the early afternoon.

When our open-backed, 2 ½ ton trucks pulled up at the parachute issue building and no one was there, we were pretty sure that this was just a drill. We felt good because we were there in well under an hour. Many of my troopers, sitting in the back of the trucks in the sun, began to snooze.

Then our new division commander, a major general, showed up and started yelling at everyone. We were all shocked because we were where we were supposed to be, ready to go, and early. The General wanted the troops to clean their weapons, check their ammunition, and other maintenance items. Then my boss, the battalion commander, stepped in. Colonel Tallman confronted the general, right there in front of me. He told the general that these troops already had clean, working weapons and their ammunition had been checked before we came out. Further, he said, infantry troops never know when they'll be able to sleep next because we never knew what the tactical situation would require of us. My troopers, said the colonel, should be sleeping now if they could; that was good preparation for combat.

When the Colonel was finished, no one said anything—and the General left. It's worthy of note that the Colonel became a general.

101st Airborne

The 101st Division headquarters was organized 2 November 1918 at Camp Shelby, Mississippi, but what demobilized the following month shortly after World War I ended.

Commonly known as "The Screaming Eagles" the 101st is most famous for their role in Operation Overlord (Normandy invasion of WW2), Operation Market Garden, the liberation of the Netherlands and action during the Battle of the Bulge around the city of Bastogne, Belgium. In Vietnam, the 101st Airborne fought in several major campaigns and battles including the fight for Hamburger Hill in May 1969.

I was thinking about...

my old first sergeant, Robert L. Cook. I took command of Company C in Jan of 1967; I was a brand new captain, newly married, and just back from a tour in Vietnam. Top, as first sergeants are called, had been in that company for nearly 15 years, except for a one-year tour in Vietnam as an advisor. He gently taught me how to run a company, and I was a pretty good student. One day I learned just how much he had taught me.

I was inspecting one of the platoons during a Saturday morning inspection—all the troops had all their equipment and other items needed for a quick deployment displayed on their bunks (this was called a junk-on-the-bunk inspection). I looked at a fresh bar of soap on a bunk and gently squeezed it; it was fine. The platoon sergeant asked me what I was doing, and I explained that back at West Point, some five or six years ago, one summer some combat troops had come in to teach us about being officers; one platoon taught us squad and platoon tactics. The sergeants later taught us how to inspect soldiers and barracks. It was explained that some troops would use a razor blade to cut out the bottom of a soap wrapper and use the soap, to avoid having to buy a new bar of soap (privates weren't paid much back in the days of the draft). The way to check this was to squeeze the bar.

It turns out, that platoon sergeant was the guy who'd taught me about squeezing soap bars; he had been a squad leader in a platoon with my now first sergeant as the platoon sergeant. Yes, they had been at West Point that summer, and they had taught me both tactics and how to do inspections.

After a few laughs, I reminded them that they'd better like the way I run the company, because they taught me how to do it. Less than a year later we deployed to Vietnam together when the entire division deployed to Vietnam, and a good company they proved to be when the chips were down.

I was thinking about…

conducting an inspection of my company in the 101st Airborne Division. Most Saturday mornings involved inspections. Some inspections were just for neatness and some involved the display of everything needed for combat. This was a junk-on-the-bunk inspection. My soldiers lived in a common bay. The sergeants who lived in the barracks lived in two-man rooms. I was inspecting a two-man room and noticed a large board behind the lockers. I asked about it. One of the sergeants, a good soldier, but one with a bit of an attitude, told me he used it for laying out tactical scenarios that he and other soldiers could work out. That sounded good, but it clearly was for dice games—and gambling was forbidden in the barracks. I spoke gently but firmly to him about this situation; it was clear that he was busted. Then I asked him if he clearly understood what I wanted him to do. After a long pause, he said, "Yes, sir." My quick response was, "Kiss your what, Sergeant?" I could tell that was what he really wanted to say from the look on his face while I was correcting him. No, he didn't say anything like that out loud. But my response caused a look on his face that said something like "I know I didn't say that out loud—did I?" After a minute I smiled and told him that, no, he didn't say it out loud—but it was written all over his face. I never had a problem with that sergeant again. Once we got out in the hall, I was afraid my First Sergeant, who was with me, was going to die laughing.

Enlisted Command Structure

E1 - Private

E2 - Private

E3 - Private 1st Class

E4 - Specialist (non-NCO)

E4 - Corporal

E5 - Sergeant

E6 - Staff Sergeant

E7 - Sergeant First Class

E8 - Master Sergeant

E8 - First Sergeant

E9 - Sergeant Major

E9 - Command Sergeant Major

E9 - Sergeant Major of the Army

I was thinking about...

when the 101st was scheduled to deploy to Vietnam in December 1967. Since that would leave a mostly empty post, Mother Army activated a basic training unit there in the fall, and new recruits, mostly draftees, began arriving for training.

One of the "other" activities at Fort Campbell was a US Navy installation called Clarksville Base. It was a fairly large ammunition storage facility surrounded by four barbed wire fences and patrolled by Marines. Each day one of the two interior fences was electrified. I never knew why the super security; most of us assumed that nuclear weapons were stored there.

Well, one evening before our unit deployed one of the new basic trainees decided he didn't like being in the army and decided to run away. He headed out after dark. When he arrived at a fence, he climbed it, knowing that Fort Campbell had a fence around it. He was shortly confronted by a second fence—and decided to climb that one, too. That's when the Marines found him. It's a good thing for that boy that it was the third fence that was hot that evening.

I was thinking about...

when I was a company commander in the 101st Airborne Division. I made it a point to meet with my senior sergeants and lieutenants every month to discuss how the company was doing and things we might do better. We usually met in the mess hall and talked for an hour or so; no subject was off limits.

For a while, I was really pleased with the great ideas I was getting from my senior NCOs, but their input slowly diminished. I was surprised as I very often took their advice and made some changes in the way we did business.

Finally, I confronted one of my platoon sergeants—a very sharp soldier and a good leader. I asked him what was happening. He clearly didn't want to answer, but I made it clear that I wasn't going to let him go until we got this out.

"Well, sir," he said, "when one of us came up with an idea that you liked, you immediately make the person who suggested it responsible for implementing it. We've learned that the more good ideas we share the more work we got. So, we stopped sharing."

I was surprised—and embarrassed. He was right. I thanked him for his honesty and changed my ways. That was just one example of the many times that good sergeants showed me how to be a better officer.

I was thinking about…

my first ever visit to the great state of Michigan—August 1967. I was a rifle company commander in the 101st Airborne Division. We had a new battalion commander who had been my company's Tactical Officer at West Point, Lieutenant Colonel Richard Tallman. I got a call at home at about 4 am telling me that we had an alert and to get into the company fast. I was sure that it was our new boss having a surprise readiness test to see how fast we could assemble; I made a mental note to chew out the sergeant for saying "alert", which is a response to an emergency, instead of saying "readiness test," which I was sure that this was. Well, it was an alert.

In the early morning of July 23, 1967, one of the worst riots in US history broke out in the heart of Detroit's predominantly African-American inner city. Michigan Governor Romney tried for a day to control things, then he asked the president for help—and in we went.

While in Detroit I never saw an angry person. My unit was located in a residential area near the rioting, and the locals were really glad we were in their neighborhood. There was one house fire in my area, a lady overloaded a wall socket.

However, some of my troops rode shotgun on fire-trucks, and they got snipped at regularly.

It was all over in about four days; 43 people were dead,

342 injured, and nearly 1,400 buildings had been burned.

When I got assigned to Grand Rapids, MI, in 1984 I was a bit nervous; then I found out that all of Michigan is not like Detroit was then.

The Detroit Riot of 1967

On Sunday at 3:45AM, July 23, 1967, Detroit police officers raided the Blind Pig (an unlicensed weekend drinking club at 9125 12th Street. Police expected only a few people inside, but instead found 82 black people celebrating the return of two local GIs from the Vietnam War. The police arrested everyone inside. While they were arranging for transportation, a large crowd of onlookers gathered on the street. The riot broke out when an onlooker threw a bottle at a police officer.

Things escalated and didn't calm down until 4 days later. 7,231 people were arrested; 1,189 people were injured; 43 people died. 2,509 stores were looted or burned, 388 families rendered homeless or displaced.

I was thinking about…

one of the most useful classes I ever attended while in the Army. I was a company commander in the 101st Airborne Division and was sent to a week-long class on maintenance of vehicles and equipment. I was sent because one of the things we officers were often assigned to do was, in teams, be sent to inspect other unit's maintenance and procedures.

Well, one day they wheeled this large trailer into the class area; it had a big collapsible tower on it; the tower had a propeller on it. No one had any idea what it was or what it did. We were then asked what we would do it we were sent to inspect a unit that had a bunch of these things. None of us had a clue. Then they opened our eyes. Yes, we all had trailers and knew how to inspect wheels, tires, hitches and the like. Good start. Then we were told to ask for the operator and ask him to get his whatever-it-was ready to operate. Finally, we'd ask him to operate it while we questioned him about how he maintained his equipment. He never had to know that we didn't know what his thing-a-ma-jig was until he explained it.

I became a bit smarter that day. Another team of sergeants had made me a better officer. By the way, the thing measured wind velocity at airfields.

I was thinking about...

a jerk I had to deal with as a company commander. The 101st Airborne Division had been alerted for deployment to Vietnam. It was now October 1967; we were to deploy in December. I had one young trooper who was a total goof off. We were in the process of having him thrown out of the army as a misfit; the paperwork was being processed. Then we were told that all troops must be granted two-weeks of pre-deployment leave. We started sending people on leave. We delayed goof-off's leave, believing that my authorization to discharge him would come down. Finally, we had to send him on leave. While he was gone the discharge paperwork did arrive.

Of course, just to show us that he would never do what we told him, he came back from his leave three days late. The first sergeant and I had discussed this. When he came in he was brought before me, and he had a smirk on his face. I produced the paperwork for his discharge and went over it with him. Then I told him that if he'd come back on time, he would have been discharged by now. And then I tore up the paperwork and threw it into my wastebasket. He was shocked beyond belief. Then his platoon sergeant and squad leader showed up. I told the goof-off that he was now going to Vietnam. Further, he was going to have the worst and most dangerous jobs available over there. Finally, if he disobeyed a single order, I'd have him court-martialed and jailed—in Vietnam.

I know I didn't have to court-martial him in Vietnam, so I guess he decided to grow up. He certainly wasn't the first, or the last, person to grow up while in uniform. Score one for the good guys.

Military Discharges

Honorable - Service members must receive a rating of good to excellent for their service.

General - Service members perform at satisfactory but not exceptional levels.

Entry Level Separation - Service members with less than 180 days in service may receive this.

Other Than Honorable - Most severe of the administrative discharge types. Typically handed down when the service member is convicted in a civilian court of a crime.

Bad Conduct - Only handed down by a Court Martial, and often follows confinement in a military correctional facility.

Dishonorable - Only handed down by a Court Martial. Reserved for what the military considers the worst crimes.

I was thinking about...

my time in Vietnam. I had little experience with a .45 caliber semi-automatic pistol before arriving in country as a second lieutenant, but I quickly found one and carried it along with my rifle. The pistol was WWII vintage and badly worn. It jammed so often I really didn't consider it reliable. When I'd loan it to a trooper who was going into a tunnel I warned him that often it was good for only one shot.

After my first Vietnam tour I was assigned to Fort Campbell, KY, where I assumed command of an airborne rifle company. My assigned weapon was, yes, a .45 pistol. It might have been the same one I'd left in Vietnam. It rattled when I fired it the parts were so worn. Then the division was ordered to deploy to Vietnam, so we all had to qualify with our weapons. For the life of me, I just couldn't hit all those bulls-eyes with my old rattley weapon. When qualifying with a rifle, the shooter shot at a silhouette, but with the pistol it was a bulls-eye target. After about a hundred tries I finally barely qualified. I deployed with my company to Vietnam—wearing that old pistol. That's why I own only revolvers today.

The 1911 Pistol

The M1911 was the standard-issue sidearm for the United States military from 1911 to 1986, when it was replaced by the 9 mm Beretta M9 pistol.

John Browning started designing the 1911 in the 1890s, and Colt manufacturing put it into production in 1911, hence the name M1911.

The M1911 shoots a 45 ACP caliber bullet and uses a 7-round detachable magazine. Over 2.7 million were manufactured, and they were the primary service pistol for World War I, World war II, the Korean War, and the Vietnam War.

The strength of the M1911 is its knock-down power. The large and heavy, slow-moving (825 feet per second) bullet created a lot of kinetic energy.

The Gillem Kids, 1950s

Big brother Denny and his three sisters

My Explorer Scout Post; I'm 3rd from the left in the front row. These are the guys with whom I learned to rappell.

Plebe Denny Gillem at West Point

Student council on US Affairs. The guest speaker was Robert Kennedy; I'm on his left.

West Point, Company E-2, first classmen (seniors) 1964. I'm in the back on the left

Ranger School--I have my hand on
old "One-Eye's" head

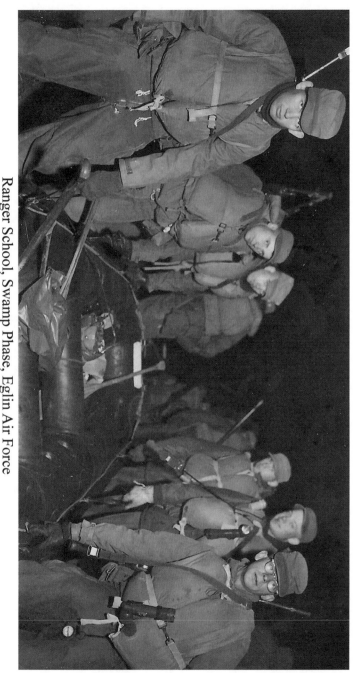

Ranger School, Swamp Phase, Eglin Air Force Base, Dec 1964; I'm on the left.

1LT Gillem, aide de camp, Vietnam 1966

Rifle platoon leader and radio operator,
Vietnam, 1965

1LT Cleo Hogan, MAJ Curt Echols, and CPT
Denny Gillem, near Hue, vietnam, Feb 1968

CPT Denny Gillem, Co C Commander and CPT Jimmy Nichols, Co B Commander, Vietnam 1968

Goeppingen, Germany; my dad, son, and I in front of my battalion headquarters.

Receiving the Bronze Star for valor from Major General
Mel Zais, CG 101st Airborne Division, Vietnam, 1968

I won. I got the most wonderful lady
in the world. She's mine.

Marilyn and I en route to the Stanford
Army ROTC Military Ball

Promotion to Major, 1970

Promotion to Lt Colonel 1979

Graduation day at Stanford with my wife, dad,
and step-mom. I received an MA in Education
(Administration)

Professor of Military Science, University of Tampa

Promotion to Lt Colonel, 1979

Lt Colonel Gillem

Marilyn and I with Navy Lt Commander Brian Harp. I was the guest speaker at the Navy Ball in Grand Rapids.

Josh Leng and I at the Michigan Association of
Broadcasters awards banquet; Frontlines of Freedom
took all available hardware

Recording Frontlines of Freedom, 2015

VIETNAM ...AGAIN

As expected, the 101st Airborne Division deployed to Vietnam in December 1967. Actually, the division's First Brigade was already there—the rest of the division deployed in December. We flew over on Air Force aircraft.

I was thinking about...

when my company, as a part of the 101st Airborne Division, deployed from Fort Campbell, KY, to Vietnam. We had shipped all our big stuff by ship and an advanced party had gone ahead of us by a couple of weeks. The division was to fly over there. Our commanding general wanted us to be ready to fight when we got off the planes in Vietnam. This made sense, since we were landing in a combat zone. However, the Air Force had rules that prohibited loaded weapons from being in their planes, and they didn't even want our troops to have ammunition for their weapons with them. This created a real challenge. My company was divided between two C-141 cargo jets which were rigged for passengers. Not only did the pilot of my aircraft see the wisdom of no armed or even possibly armed passengers on his plane, he out-ranked me. Fortunately for me, as he and I discussed the situation, including landing at Ben Hoa Air Force Base in Vietnam, we agreed that all ammunition would be packed in sealed boxes inside our aircraft. One-half-hour before we were to land the boxes could be broken open and ammunition distributed to all the troops. Of course, no weapons would be loaded until we were out of the aircraft. The pilot of the other aircraft carrying my company agreed with our plan, and everything worked well. A little cross-Service cooperation worked again.

By the way, all was peaceful around us when we landed, but I was very happy to have all my troops armed and ready to go.

The M16 Rifle

At the outset of the Vietnam War, the M14 was issued as the standard service rifle. However, while it had good knock-down power, it was difficult to control on full auto, and the ammo was too heavy to carry in large quantity.

The M16 reached Vietnam in 1963 and suffered from reliabillity problems. The ammo (5.56mm) was smaller and lighter, but the rifle didn't hold up well to the wet jungle environment. A forward assist and chrome plated bore were added along with a 30-round magazine, and the M16A1 replaced the M14 by 1969.

The M16 has a 20-inch barrel with a muzzle velocity of 3,110 feet per second. The maximum effective range is 601 yards. It has a sustained rate of fire at 12 to 15 rounds per minute, and a cyclic rate of fire of 700–950 rounds per minute.

Even though the M16A1 corrected the reliability problems, the reputation of the rifle continues to suffer.

I was thinking about…

my time as a rifle company commander in Vietnam. It was during the intense fighting that began with the North Vietnamese attacks during Tet on 31 Jan 1968. We were fighting almost daily for weeks and were looking pretty scruffy. I'd written my dad and asked him to find some hand clippers that would cut hair. They came and shortly thereafter my company was assigned to secure a base camp for three days. While regular patrolling and perimeter security was non-stop, it was a time to relax and do some maintenance. I called all the available troops together and let them know that, yes, they were all as clean as I'd see them in some time, but I wanted all the facial hair gone and for all of them to cut their hair. I then sat my first sergeant on a 5-gallon water can in front of them, and I cut his hair. If you're interested, that was the first time in my life I'd ever cut hair, so, yes, it was bad, but it was short. I then volunteered to cut any soldier's hair who couldn't find a way to get rid of the long locks.

This may shock you, but no one asked me to cut their hair.

I want to share a story…

that one of my guests, a West Point classmate, Ian Carter pulled out of my memory. Ian wrote a book about the Tet Offensive in 1968 in Vietnam. I was a rifle company commander in the 101st Airborne Division during that fight. One afternoon we were conducting a battalion frontal attack across 50 or 100 yards of open rice paddy against a dug in enemy. This was the biggest attack by far that I was ever in. Three companies attacked in the open. There were machine guns firing and artillery and mortars and lots of rifle and grenades. It was a "Hollywood typical" attack. There were two companies on line, including my Company C; maybe 300 soldiers total. The other company on line, Company B, had in it a very sharp, very popular sergeant who was Hispanic and had a very distinctive accent. We were half-way across this field, noise everywhere, bullets flying—when across the field comes a cry, "Aieeeeee! My babies!" The voice was definitely the sergeant's. The result was a giggle that went up and down the line of attacking troops. I can still remember clearly that giggle while in the middle of the most horrendous attack I'd ever participated in. Yes, we won the fight, and it turns out the good sergeant was hit in a very sensitive spot by a dud rifle grenade. Yes, he got kidded a lot, later.

I was thinking about...

a day—actually, a night—in Vietnam. We'd been in a major fight the day before. That day my company swept the northern part of a wooded area that the enemy had been using. We set up a defensive position for the night at the northern-most point. There were some trenches already dug there; it was a natural defensive site that had likely been used off and on for decades. That night it rained; it rained hard. And, the enemy, from somewhere out in the dark, in another tree-line, started firing rockets at us. Between the dark and the rain, the rockets weren't hurting us much, but it was darned scary. I let the battalion operations center know that we were under fire and that I'd give them an update once I figured out what was really going on. A few minutes later a really big rocket came in right near me; apparently it landed in a very wet trench and just slid—sort of slurped— down it until it ran out of trench. It didn't go off; I'm not sure why. Well, by now my leaders and I had figured out that it was rocket fire only, and we knew about where it was coming from. I called battalion on the radio to give an update and to request air strikes.

The young radio operator who took my report was clearly writing down everything I said on some kind of a report form.

Then he asked me exactly what size rockets were coming in. I told him that I wasn't sure. Next, I told him about the one that had landed near me and was in a wet trench nearby. He said he needed to know the size of that rocket. I asked him if he really wanted me, the company commander of a company taking enemy fire, to leave my foxhole and find the trench and crawl down it until I found the rocket, then to use my flash-light to confirm the size of the rocket, all the while hoping it didn't just go off. He said that he had to have the size of that rocket. At that point I told him I wanted to talk personally to the battalion operations officer, a major. When the major came on he laughed at my story, told me the radio operator was a new guy taking his job very seriously. The major did call for the air strikes, which didn't come, because of the weather. However, we eventually received artillery support which did cause the rockets to stop.

I still occasionally think about crawling down that muddy trench in the rain seeking to find a dud rocket and identify it. Now, it's funny.

I was thinking about...

the time I was a rifle company commander in the 101st Airborne Division. At that time every company had a company clerk. One of that person's main jobs each duty day was to type out a morning report which listed all changes in personnel status. That document had to be totally accurate with no corrections (we didn't have computers in those days—heck, not even electric typewriters). We were blessed to have a great company clerk. Since we were an airborne company, and getting parachute qualified required volunteering, we were all volunteers (this was in the days of the draft). Our company clerk decided that he didn't really like jumping out of airplanes in flight, so he found ways to minimize the number of times he had to jump; that was fine with the first sergeant and me. He had to jump once a quarter to maintain jump status—and parachute pay; this he did. Once our unit deployed to Vietnam we were told that we no longer had to do any jumps, and we would still get our jump-pay. Our clerk was a happy guy. Then, after about six months our division was re-designated as an airmobile division; this means that we were now helicopter mobile, not airborne. At that time we began to get replacements who were not parachute qualified.

At this point, our wonderful clerk asked to be taken off jump status and to be able to withdraw from being parachute qualified. He really liked the company, but he really didn't want to ever be assigned to an airborne unit again. I suggested that he wait until he rotated home before dropping his jump status. Dropping now would cost him the $55 per month jump pay he was getting, but he didn't want to take any chances. So a non-airborne, straight-leg he became. But he remained a great clerk.

Parachute History

The earliest known reference to parachute development dates back to the Renaissance period in 1470AD.

In the late 18th century the modern parachute was invented by Louis-Sébastien Lenormand in France, who made the first recorded public jump in 1783.

The first military use of the parachute was by artillery observers on tethered observation balloons in World War I.

I was thinking about...

eating C-Rations. I ate a lot of them in my two years in Vietnam. Some of the stuff they packed into those cans was pretty gross, but I could eat all of it—except "Ham and Lima Beans;" that I couldn't handle. The secret to enjoying C-Rats was, at least for me, a bottle of hot sauce and either a container of onion salt or, if possible, a fresh onion. Dump both on generously and heat her up—and yum, yum. You may not know this but plastic explosive C4 burns rather nicely. A small piece of it and a match and it's chow time. If the circumstances required me to eat the meal cold, then often I didn't eat all of it. The new field chow, Meals Ready to Eat, or MREs, are delicious compared to C-Rats. The troops have it easy now—I know, all old soldiers say that.

I remembered that...

after my company had been in Vietnam for about four months I was hurt; when I got out of the hospital a few days later the decision had been made to transfer me to division headquarters where I would work on the G-3 (operations) staff in the Tactical Operations Center (TOC). I ended up running the night shift, keeping track of all tactical operations going on throughout the (about 18,000 man) division. While there I met the Division Aviation Officer, a major who was, obviously, a pilot. He had just come from an assignment as the personal pilot for a four-star general in Vietnam. This general had decided he wanted to be able to fly himself and got himself sent to flight school (probably an abbreviated version) and came back a qualified pilot. Nonetheless, he was not permitted to fly except when accompanied by a certified instructor-pilot, which my friend was. One day the general got to the chopper before my friend and had it running.

A word of insight here. When flying a helicopter, the tail rotor's pitch is controlled by two pedals on the floor. There's no resistance to the pedals; you can push either of these pedals to the floor with your finger.

Okay, the general is in the pilot's seat, and he complains

that the foot pedals are sticky; there is something wrong with them. My friend asks the general to take both feet off the pedals, and the general does. Now he told the general to put one foot on one of the pedals; the general did, and it went right to the floor; there was nothing wrong with it. It seems our good general was so nervous about flying that his legs were tense and he was pushing down with both feet at the same time; he was resisting himself.

It's always nice to have a funny story to tell about a senior officer.

Helicopters in Vietnam

The helicopter was used during the Vietnam War more extensively than any other time to date. Because of Vietnam's jungle canopy and lack of a sophisticated road system, the helicopter was needed more than ever for jobs like transporting supplies and troops, evacuating wounded, aerial reconnaissance and as gunships in support of ground troops.

A random thought…

I've logged well over a thousand hours in helicopters, most of them in Vietnam. The trips were everything from med-evacs, to logistic hauls, to combat assaults. I even have some stick time flying one. You know that I was in a helicopter crash over there. My degree from West Point was in engineering. I can explain, technically, why and how a helicopter—a rotary wing aircraft--can fly. That said, I really don't believe those things can really fly. They must do it with mirrors. What do you think?

How Helicopters Fly

This quote by famous broadcast journalist, Harry Reasoner in 1971, sums up my attitude on helicopters and flight.

"An airplane by its nature wants to fly. ... A helicopter does not want to fly. It is maintained in the air by a variety of forces and controls working in opposition to each other, and if there is any disturbance in this delicate balance, the helicopter stops flying, immediately and disastrously. There is no such thing as a gliding helicopter."

FORT KNOX, U OF TEXAS AT EL PASO, ARMED FORCES STAFF COLLEGE

When I returned from my second tour in Vietnam I was school bound. As an infantry officer I'd been selected to go to the Armor Officers Advanced Course at Fort Knox; this was an honor. From there I was sent to get my master's degree (in political science) at the University of Texas at El Paso; I was promoted to the rank of major while I was there. For my next assignment I went to Stanford University where I served in the Army ROTC Department and also earned another master's degree. My next stop was as a student at the Armed Forces Staff College in Norfolk, VA.

I was thinking about...

my tour at Fort Knox, Kentucky. At the time, Fort Knox was the home of the Army's Armor Branch. It was an honor for me, as an infantryman, to be selected to attend the Armor Branch's Advanced Course located there (most of my infantry peers were sent to the Infantry Officers Advanced Course at Fort Benning). Back then, the advanced course was a nine-month training for captains and junior majors, to prepare them for service on the staffs of higher commands. There were well over a hundred students in my class; about 20 were infantrymen. We banded together so we could pick on the armor guys. I helped devise a game of Spring-Butt-Bingo. Each student who wanted to play got a standard bingo card—five boxes high and five boxes wide. In each box he could write the name of one of our classmates; no single classmate's name could be used more than twice. Each time a student raised his hand to ask a question in class (and was called on by the instructor), it was like calling a number in bingo; if you had his name on your card you could fill it in. The first student to get cover-all bingo had to stand up and ask a question with a phrase we had designed. The phrase would be something like "tanks are too slow" or "infantry leads the way." That would end that game; one of us would walk over to that student and give him his prize. Despite my goofing off, I did graduate on the Commandant's List.

Tanks and Warfare

The armored car was the forerunner of the tank, but it wasn't suitable for warfare because it needed smooth roads. The first tanks were developed during WWI to solve the stalemate of trench warfare.

The primitive tanks of WWI had trouble in the mud and it took time to improve the design and to develop workable tactics of this new weapon. Because of this, it achieved mixed success in WWI.

It wasn't until WWII that the tank proved its mettle, and went on to change modern warfare forever.

I was thinking about...

my days at Fort Knox, Kentucky. It was an honor for me, as an infantryman, to be selected to attend the Armor Branch's Advanced Course located there. I was just back from my second Vietnam tour; while on that tour I was selected for promotion to the rank of major. As a result, while I was still a captain, I was provided with major's quarters at Fort Knox; they were quite nice. I really enjoyed the training and the social time to get to know many of my peers. The army was trying some new things, including a Junior Officers' Council on the post. I was selected to be on it; we junior folks could provide some input to the brass. We didn't do much, but it was cool to be on the council.

Then we came to the time when the course was over and it was time to move out of our government quarters. There were a number of sergeants who worked for the post with the duty of issuing and clearing quarters. When we left post these sergeants would inspect the quarters to ensure that they were left clean for the next occupant. Most of these sergeants had wives who were in the business of cleaning quarters for those folks who wished to hire a cleaning team. My wife and I decided to clean our own quarters; we should have noticed that every place that had a cleaning team was cleared immediately. Well, the sergeant came by and looked until he found something not clean enough, and he left. We cleaned it, and scheduled another inspection. He came back and looked until he found something else. At this point the racket became clear, and I was really, really glad to be on the Junior Officers Council. One call to the brass and suddenly my quarters were cleared. I suspect, but don't know, that the sergeant's little squeeze play was over. They should have gone to jail, in my opinion. I'll never know.

Fort Knox

Fort Knox is an army base located south of Louisville, Kentucky. For most civilians, Fort Knox is synonymous for the United States Bullion Depository operated by the US Treasury.

But Fort knox, comprising 119,000 acres was the US Army Armor school for 60 years. The General George Patton Museum in also located at Fort Knox.

The US Army Armor school is now located at Fort Benning, Georgia

I was thinking about...

Fort Knox. A good friend of mine was stationed there a few years after I left. The Army had been working on a new tank. There had been cost over-runs and all kinds of problems. The media was calling on the Army to junk the tank. And then everything worked. The final fixes on the tank were all that were needed, and that baby rocked. About ten tanks had been out in the field at Fort Knox for a couple of weeks doing a final test; they were coming in that day. Everything had worked perfectly. The media was notified, and my friend was assigned to escort a TV anchorman and his camera man. They had a tank that was just coming in from the field test pull up so they could see it. The anchorman stood on the back deck of the tank and began speaking. Basically, what he said was this tank was a piece of over-priced junk and nothing worked on it. The tank commander, who was just a few feet from him on the tank, turned to him and said, "Excuse me, sir, but what you just said was wrong. This tank works great." The anchor had the camera turned off and turned to the sergeant. He was very nice. He told the sergeant that, just like in the Army, he had senior people that he reported to, and he did what they told him to do. Then the anchor said that he was told to come down here and say that the tank was a piece of junk, and that's what he was going to do. The sergeant's response was, "Get off my tank."

He did get off. My friend wasn't sure how the anchor got off the tank, because my buddy was laying on the ground laughing.

M1 Abrams Battle Tank

Named after General Creighton Abrams, former Army Chief of Staff and Commander of U.S. military forces in the Vietnam War from 1968 to 1972, the M1 tank entered service in 1980 as a replacement for the M60.

The Abrams is armed with:

- 105 mm L/52 M68 rifled gun (55 rounds)

- 1 × .50-caliber (12.7 mm) M2HB heavy machine gun with 900 rounds

- 2 × 7.62 mm (.308 in) M240 machine guns with 10,400 rounds

The initial Abrams was upgraded to the M1A1 and then to the M1A2. It is still the main battle tank of the US Army and the US Marine Corps.

I was thinking about...

my time at the University of Texas at El Paso. The Army assigned me to UTEP to get a Masters in Political Science with a focus on International Relations. I'd been out of school for five years and had spent two year in Vietnam, so I wasn't sure how well I'd do back in the academic world. Most of my peers were kids who'd just finished their bachelor's degree, had not left academia, and had not been in the real world. I found that my maturity made up for my rusty study habits. Anyway, I was approaching the point where I was going to have to present and defend my thesis, and I was, well, nervous. I wasn't sure how to prepare. I found a fellow student closer to my age who seemed to be a perpetual student. He was married and had a job, but stayed in school. I asked him if he'd be willing to tutor me. He was willing, and asked if I could teach him calculus. He was going to need it for something in his program. Since my undergraduate degree from West Point was in engineering and I'd had lots of math, I agreed. I went to the Math Department and asked around until I found a professor who had a number of extra calculus books; he gave me one. I took it home, sat down and opened it. I couldn't even get through chapter 1; it was all Greek to me. After several false starts, I gave up. I went to my friend and told him that I must have done an extra good job of flushing the knowledge I had gained in college, because I couldn't help him at all. I did give him the text book. He was so pleased to get the free book that he said he'd teach himself, and still mentor me. It worked; I survived the thesis defense and got my degree.

The moral of this story is, if you want help in calculus, ask someone else.

What is Calculus?

According to dictionary.com
calculus - [kal-kyuh-luh s]

noun, plural calculi [kal-kyuh-lahy]

1. a method of calculation, especially one of several highly systematic methods of treating problems by a special system of algebraic notations, as differential or integral calculus.

If you can readily understand this, then drop down and give me 50 push-ups. You deserve it!

I was thinking about…

our time in El Paso. The Army had sent me to the University of Texas at El Paso for graduate school. We were fortunate to be able to rent a home a block from the school. It was also very close to the border with Mexico, and it was not uncommon for homes to be burglarized in our area. One day it happened to us. The house was a bit of a mess and some things were missing. I called the police. Shortly thereafter there was a knock on our front door. I opened the door to a police officer—and it shocked the heck out of me. When I was a company commander in the 101st Airborne Division I had a great mess sergeant named Isaac LaFrance. The officer facing me had a nametag saying LaFrance, and he looked just like my mess sergeant. Yes, it was his twin brother. We had a very enjoyable talk after he completed his report. The criminal was never caught.

I was thinking about...

    our first winter in El Paso. I was there attending graduate school at the university. To make an understatement, they don't get much snow in El Paso. One day it snowed; it really snowed. There was about two inches on the streets. We lived on the main street that ran from downtown past the university. It was uphill from the center of the city; we lived at the top of the hill. While my wife and I were familiar with driving in snow, few other people were. The city was at somewhat of a standstill. Of course, there were many brave souls who had to get somewhere, despite the snow. Folks from downtown were coming up the hill at either 2 mph or 92 mph. It was confusion. The first major collision took place in front of our house. I called the police and sat back to watch the demolition derby.

I was thinking about...

snow. About two hours north of El Paso is Ruidoso, New Mexico. There's a nice big mountain there and some very good skiing in the winter. Bob was stationed at the Army ROTC unit at UTEP; he and his wife, Jan, were among our closest friends. We all liked the idea of skiing, but none of us were great skiers. On one occasion we were skiing at Ruidoso. We were at the top of the mountain and had selected a somewhat easy route to ski down. Bob led; Marilyn followed, then Jan; I was the tail gunner. We were skiing down a very narrow valley. The trail was maybe ten feet wide with vertical walls of snow on both sides. I was watching Jan—when she disappeared. I stopped, blinked, took off my goggles and looked again. I could see Marilyn and Bob well ahead of me, but no Jan. There was nowhere she could have gone. As I moved slowly down the trail I saw a, well, an irregularity. Jan had somehow made a 90 degree left turn and had penetrated about five feet into the snow bank. She didn't know where she was and was quite shaken; I grabbed her and pulled her out. Needless to say, I was very appreciated that day. Further, needless to say, we relived that event on more than one occasion in the future. I like rescuing beautiful women.

I was remembering...

a friend we made when we were stationed in El Paso. Fort Bliss, Texas, is also located there. It was the home of the Air Defense Artillery, and foreign officers came there to be trained. We volunteered to sponsor one of these officers. Uli was a German Air Force officer in his young twenties. He was fun to be with, and a bit wild. On one occasion he and some of his fellow Germans decided to go across the border into Juarez, Mexico. While there they apparently consumed a number of adult beverages. When they were driving back across the border, a US Customs Agent asked them their nationalities and what, if anything, they were bringing into the US. Uli answered, "We are Russians, and we bring machine-guns." As you might expect, the world came down on them. It took Uli about two days to get back to Fort Bliss and back into his classes. He thought it was a great time. Ah, youth...

I was thinking about...

the first class I took at the University of Texas at El Paso in my master's program. The professor was the president emeritus of the University and was a very bright and likeable man. The grade for his course was determined by our only project, a lengthy paper. At the semester's end we each had an appointment with him for a critique. When I came in he said some nice things about my approach and analysis. I still remember his final words. "If you ever get important, Mr. Gillem, be sure to get a secretary who can spell." That was my motivation to work on the mechanics of writing.

STAFF COLLEGE

In the army, an officer who was competitive for promotion was selected to attend the Command and General Staff College (CGSC) at Fort Leavenworth, KS, as a major. Some officers were sent to the equivalent schools of the other services; the multi-service (called "Joint" in military talk) equivalent was the Armed Forces Staff College at Norfolk, VA; I attended this college in 1973. It was interesting to get to know officers from the other services and learn to work together.

I was thinking about...

the Chief of Staff of the Armed Forces Staff College (AFSC) a very tough Marine Colonel. He was all business and never smiled. We students were all happy that our normal duties did not have us around him. One weekend we had a costume party and dance; the Colonel came as a total hippy. He had long hair (a wig), peace symbols, tattoos, etc., and, strangest of all, a big smile. Literally everyone was standing and gawking at him, and he was lovin' it. I can still close my eyes and see his costume and smirk.

I remember being quite proud of this…

One of the things that galled many AFSC students was that those among us who were pilots were getting flight pay (over $100/month, as I remember) while being students. There were many loud "discussions" about it at the Officers Club. There was an active Toastmasters Club at the college, and I was a member. One meeting when it was my turn to speak I announced that my subject would be to support flight pay for our pilot students. This shocked everyone because I'm not a pilot. The punch line in my talk was that while I felt they should get their flight pay while here as students, they clearly should not get their base pay. Even the pilots applauded.

I was thinking about…

our time at Norfolk. As the AFSC was adjacent to the US Navy Base at Norfolk, on one occasion our class was given a tour of a submarine that had just come in to port. It was one of our most modern nuclear subs. As it turns out, one of our classmates was an exchange officer from the British Navy. He'd just come from commanding the sister ship of this sub; we do sell our stuff to the British. However, he was not allowed on the boat because he didn't have a US security clearance. We were all pretty sure the real reason was that we didn't provide to the British all of our secret stuff, and he'd recognize what was missing. Either way, it was a fun tour.

I was remembering...

a surprise birthday party I had for Marilyn while we were at Norfolk. She had warned me the year before, when she turned the big three-zero, that there would be no big deal for her birthday. I understood the instructions and complied with them. However, while we were at Norfolk she had her thirty-first birthday. I had everyone over for a surprise "Over Thirty" birthday party. Guest brought "old folks" stuff, like crutches and support hose, etc. It was a fun time. I didn't get in too much trouble.

Armed Forces Staff College

During WWII, it was discovered that few officers were prepared to lead in joint action by ground, sea, and air forces. For that reason, the AFSC was established in 1947 in Norfolk, Virginia.

It's stated mission was to educate national security professionals in the planning and execution of joint, multinational, and interagency operations in order to instill a primary commitment to joint, multinational, and interagency teamwork, attitudes, and perspectives.

On October 30th 2000, President Bill Clinton signed the Defense Authorization Bill which renamed the AFSC to Joint Forces Staff College.

Stanford & the University of Tampa – ROTC Faculty

I served as the XO (Executive Officer or second-in-command) of the Military Science (Army ROTC) Department for most of my 2 ½ years at Stanford; later I was assigned as the PMS (Professor of Military Science—or commander) of the Army ROTC unit at the University of Tampa. I'm combining these two experiences.

I was thinking about...

the time I was an Assistant Professor of Military Science at Stanford University; that was in the early 1970s, and we were in the process of closing the unit. Because of anti-Vietnam-War protests the University told us to phase out the program. ROTC cadets attend a 6-week summer camp the summer after their junior year. The camp was held at Fort Lewis in Washington State. I was on the camp cadre both summers I was at Stanford. I had never been to Fort Lewis before. The first time I drove up there I was awed by the beauty of the place; it's clear, lush, and green. The whole northern skyline of Fort Lewis is Mount Rainier.

I quickly learned that the troops at Fort Lewis used Mount Rainier to forecast the weather. One went outside and looked north. If you couldn't see the mountain—it was raining. If you could see the mountain—it was gonna rain. Yes, it rained a lot.

I guess I'm a slow learner; a couple of years ago my sisters and I and our spouses spent a week together on the Pacific Coast not too far from Mount Rainier, and in one week we had one sunny day.

I was thinking about...

when I was a major and assigned to the Stanford University Army ROTC unit. I had to go to an all-day meeting at the not-too-far-away Presidio of San Francisco. I got there early and parked my car in a parking lot in front of the building. The parking lot was next to the post's parade ground. I spent the day in the building and came out at four pm to find a parade being set up and the parking lot empty. My car was gone. I called the military police and asked about my car. I was informed that it had been parked in a no parking area and had been towed. The MPs also offered to come get me and take me to my car, and give me a ticket for illegal parking.

I got to the MP station and asked what this was all about. I was told that the parking lot I had parked in was a no-parking area after noon as they were preparing for a parade that evening, and my car was towed. I asked how I was to know that it was a no-parking area after noon; that caused a pause. The senior MP officer, a lieutenant, agreed that there was no sign on the lot, but he said it had been in the post's daily bulletin for a week, and all post personnel were responsible to know what was in that bulletin. I agreed that post personnel were responsible to know that information, but that I was not stationed there. My question remained; how was I to know? The MP lieutenant was then facing a rather big, getting unhappy and assertive, and highly decorated major—that's me. I told him that if he couldn't resolve this in my favor then I wanted to see the post commander, and I wanted to see him now. Guess what. I didn't get the ticket. I wonder if a more junior person would have; that would have been unfair. Anyway… I drove home.

Fort Lewis

Originally, Fort Lewis was an army base, and was located 9 miles southwest of Tacoma, Washington. It was established in 1917, but is now a joint Air force/Army base and is called Joint Base Lewis–McChord.

In present times, Joint Base Lewis-McChord is a training and mobilization center for all military services and is the only Army power-projection base west of the Rocky Mountains. Its unique, geographic location provides rapid access to the deep-water ports of Seattle, Olympia and Tacoma, for deploying equipment

I was thinking about...

my assignment to the ROTC unit at Stanford University. Just before I arrived, in Feb of 1971, the university had decided to end their relationships with their ROTC units; we were, to use my term, thrown off campus. There were Army, Navy, and Air Force ROTC units at Stanford; we were to phase out and be gone by June of 73. The environment was not, shall we say, totally military friendly. The big challenge was the conduct of outside military training. Younger cadets were normally trained by more senior cadets, and we now had no freshmen and would have none in the future. So I approached the local Army Reserves and National Guard units; our cadets were able to do their training with them as "acting 2nd lieutenants," or "3rd lieutenants" as we called them. The training, obviously, was realistic and challenging. Not only did this concept fit our needs, but the idea was picked up by the Army for use throughout the Army ROTC program.

I was thinking about...

my days at the Stanford University Army ROTC program. When Stanford asked the Army, Navy, and Air Force ROTC units to disband, the Air Force left almost immediately. I got to know the Navy ROTC team quite well. One of the nicest people I've ever met was the head of that program—and I'll never forget his name. He was a naval aviator named Captain John Duck.

I was thinking about...

the birth of our son. We'd been married four years and did want to have children. I came home from summer camp one lovely day to find out that we were going to have a child. I remember being told that there are three things that, regardless of the preparations one makes, you're never prepared for. One is getting married; while I see the truth of this statement, Marilyn and I adjusted to each other quite nicely. Number two is the birth of your first child—holy cow, was that right on. We had no idea how much our lives would change. Fortunately, while we weren't very near family, we had lots of good friends, mostly military friends, around us to mentor us. So our son was born in the midst of all the radicals at Stanford University Hospital. Number three, if you're interested, is starting your own business; I've done that, and it is difficult, but nothing compared to the first child.

I was thinking about…

snow skiing. Marilyn and I liked to ski and while we were at Stanford it was only a couple of hours to several fine ski areas. When Marilyn first "started showing" with our soon-to-be born son, it was skiing season. We went and had a good time.   Marilyn found that by standing up straight her weight was forward just enough for good skiing; that said, after one or two times down the slope, she decided to spend the rest of the day in the lodge. That was our last skiing trip that season.

I was remembering…

the nice family that we sponsored while we were at Stanford. One of the things the military community did was to provide sponsors for the families of military folks who were Prisoners of War or Missing in Action. We sponsored the family of Navy pilot Dick Stratton. They were a great family—and strong; they taught us things about enduring under great stress. The joy of all joys was to be there when the POWs were released and Dick came home. I still get tears in my eyes when I remember that day.

My Son - David Gillem

Our son Dave was also "California born" while I was stationed with the Army ROTC unit at Stanford University. We moved to Grand Rapids as he entered 7th grade. Dave is the undisputed athlete in the family and played soccer and basketball in high school and college. He now plays in several "over 40" soccer leagues. Presently, he is well into a successful career as a police officer, a sergeant in the Grand Rapids Police Department, and enjoys life as an assistant high school varsity girls soccer coach.

BACK IN ROTC

It was about seven years after we left Stanford that I found myself back in ROTC; these were great assignments.

I was thinking about…

arriving at the University of Tampa; I was to run the Army ROTC program. My predecessor had somehow arranged to have a 40-foot rappelling tower built on one end of the football stadium's field. It had a level at 20-feet for training beginners. I got there at the beginning of the summer, so I had no cadets and was able to look around a lot. I had a nine-year-old son who was quite active. He was with me one day when I was looking at that tower; he asked me to teach him how to rappel. I thought about it and did it. I got him up to the top of the 20-foot tower, tied him into a proper seat, and had him back over the side—20 feet in the air. It was then I remembered that when someone is rappelling there must be someone on the ground below them. This person can, by pulling on the rope on which the rappeller is descending, slow or stop his descent. But there was no one but me, and I was on top of the tower. So, out of options, I let my only son go. It turns out he weighed so little that he couldn't overcome the friction of the rope through the snap-link, and he didn't move. I quickly descended, got a hold of the rope and was able to work him down; he loved it. That was a day of real growth in my prayer life. My son ended up a top-notch rappeller; he surely doesn't have my fear of heights.

I was thinking about...

when I was running the Army ROTC unit at the University of Tampa. I'd occasionally go around the state and visit high school Junior Army ROTC units, particularly if they were having a field day of some sort. One unit was having a challenge day, and many high school ROTC-type units were competing in physical fitness, rifle marksmanship, and the like. It was a warm, Spring day. I was asked to judge push-ups; my duties were simple. If the student did a good push-up—all the way down, then all the way up, it counted. Most students started doing good push-ups, but they got sloppier and sloppier as they became tired, so it was a bit challenging. I think that's why they put me on this job. I was the highest ranking guy around and wouldn't be challenged. It almost worked. One young man, I think from a junior Marine unit, started doing push-ups, but he did the push-ups from the waist—his hips and legs weren't moving. So, I was counting "no," "no," "no." Finally I stopped him and explained that he wasn't doing regulation push-ups. He disagreed. So, in my dress uniform, I got down on the ground and showed him what was correct and what he was doing. I won the argument.

The other day...

I saw some of those mascots—the kind high school and colleges use at ball games. There are real people inside a big, cartoon-like costume. Well, that reminded me of when I had to chew out one of those cartoon-costumed people—in public. I was the head of the Army ROTC unit at the University of Tampa in the early 1980s, and there was a big parade in town. We had a cadet organization, I think it was the drill team, in the parade. They were marching in uniform with rifles. I was in uniform, walking behind or beside them.

One of these cartoon-people was out doing his thing along the parade route, when he decided to go pick on the cadets. He'd stand in their way; then he'd poke at this cadet or that one. Then he started trying to grab rifles. That did it.

I went up to him and asked him to stop. He did silly things to make me look like a fool. Then he reached for another cadet's rifle. I burst into the space between the goofball and the cadet and told him that if he even looked like he was going to touch one of those government weapons again, I'd take him out, and then have him arrested. I told him that I didn't know how to take the costume head off, so I just might take his head off in the process. There was a long moment of silence—then he danced away, doing all he could do to make me look like a fool—but he never came back.

And, yeah, I would have taken him out. I'm not sure how Mother Army would have reacted to that.

ROTC

ROTC was created by the Morrel Act of 1862. The Reserve Officers' Training Corps (ROTC) is a college-based officer training program for training commissioned officers of the United States Armed Forces. The ROTC program supplies the army with the bulk of its officer corps.

To be considered for ROTC, the candidate must meet these requirements:
- U.S. citizen
- High school diploma or equivalent
- Between ages 17 and 27
- College GPA of at least 2.5
- Army physical fitness standard

I was thinking about…

my time as the Professor of Military Science at the University of Tampa. As a Department Chair, I sat with other Department chairs on the Provost's council. Well, political correctness was doing its thing, even back in the early 1980s, and we were told that from now on we could no longer use the title of chairman or chairwoman—that was racist or sexist or something. From now on we'd have to be chair-persons. We all felt that was a bit foolish, but we also realized that the decision had been made by those way above us. One gent, I think he chaired the Biology Department, declared that he absolutely would never have a horrible title like chair-person. So, he announced to us all, from that point on he would use the title of Chair-Creature, and indeed he did—on business cards and everything.

As a result of that experience, I now use the term Chair-critter or Congress-critter, etc . I really like the term.

GERMANY

After graduating from the Armed Forces Staff College in Norfolk, VA, I was assigned to Germany. I was going back to the First Infantry Division. After a few months as the S-3 (Operations and Training Officer) of the 1st Battalion, 26th Infantry, I became the battalion XO (second in command) for the remainder of our three year tour there.

I was thinking about...

our trip to Germany. We flew, of course, on a chartered airliner full of troops and families. About half way across the Atlantic the airplane's heater broke. To say it got cold in the plane was an understatement. All the plane's crew could offer was not-enough-of those little airplane blankets. We got one to share. Our son was not quite two and had a full-body cold-weather coat with a hood, which we zipped him into; he was fine. Then I let him sleep on my chest, and he kept me warm. All Marilyn got was the flimsy blanket. But we survived.

I was thinking about...

my time in Germany as a mechanized infantry battalion XO. One of my responsibilities was the battalion's mess hall (also called a dining facility).   The mess hall was being inspected one day. While the battalion mess sergeant was there conducting the inspector around, I was there, too. At one point the inspecting officer was offered a cup of coffee. He accepted, and in jest, I think, said the coffee tasted like Yak urine.

There was an awkward silence for about 15 seconds before everyone saw the smirk on his face and all laughed. I just had to ask. "Sir," I said, "how would you know what Yak urine tasted like?"   His response, "Dennis, in desperate times men do desperate things." That got a laugh, too. And, yes, we passed the inspection.

I was thinking about…

our battalion's daily conditioning runs while I was stationed in Germany. My battalion was located at Cooke Barracks in Goeppingen. This had been a German Army base during WWII and had a small airfield. There was virtually no air traffic into or out of Cooke Barracks. About the only thing we used that airfield for was Physical Training (PT) runs in the morning. Something the post commander did to build relationships with the local community was to allow the local sheep herders to graze their flocks on the field. Avoiding sheep-dip while running in the mornings became a major effort. It was also worth a laugh when I saw lamb for sale in the post commissary (grocery store); the lamb was from New Zealand.

Back when I was...

a battalion XO in Germany I knew that our brigade's mission was as a part of the strategic reserve for US Army in Europe. This was during the Cold War, and we (as a part of NATO) were there to keep the Communists from attacking into western Europe. While no one really knows how any battle will go once the first shot is fired, we have to have plans for how we think things might go. So, I asked the military intelligence folks which enemy unit we might face first, should the war start and go as they think it might. It took a while, but they got back to me with the guess that the first unit we would meet would be the 123rd Motorized Rifle Regiment of the East German Army. That was good. Then, I asked for the names and biographies of the senior commanders in that regiment. This took a longer time before they came back with the names of the regimental commander and his battalion commanders. Interestingly enough, all of these officers had the same first name: Fnu. Now, I thought that was quite strange; actually, I was surprised that the intelligence guys hadn't thought it strange. So, I pressed them to look into it. Long story short: FNU stands for First Name Unknown.

I was thinking about…

when we were stationed in Germany. My wife's family came over to visit us—her mom and dad and her baby sister, who was maybe 15. My wife's brothers were all in college. We traveled a lot and, among other places, visited Vienna in Austria. There is a big statue of Mozart in one of the squares; he's holding a baton—you know, for leading music. I convinced my young sister-in-law that what he was holding was a beer-can opener. Beer is rather popular in that part of the world, and she was a bit in awe of all the beer, so it was easy to convince her. I don't remember how she learned the truth, but, can you believe it, she picked on me for a couple of days after that. As a matter of fact, she still picks on me.

I've been really blessed to be very close to all of my wife's family. They're great people, every one of them.

I was remembering...

a trip back to the States that we took about half-way through our tour in Europe. Marilyn's brother was graduating from the US Air Force Academy, and I was invited to commission him. We "hopped" (took a free space-available) a plane back to the States and got to Colorado Springs from there. After the ceremony, Marilyn and our son were going to spend some time with her family; I had to get back because my battalion was going into the field for a major exercise. I was sure I could "hop" from the east coast to Europe, but I needed to get there, and really didn't want to have to pay the big bucks for an airline ticket. Well, the speaker at the graduation was the Secretary of the Air Force, and he came in his own Air Force plane. I went to the Air Force Base where the plane landed and asked if I could catch a free ride on his plane—a normal thing in most cases. What I was told was that he said "no" when he found out that I was Army, not Air Force. I'll never know for sure, but I ended up buying a ticket.

I was thinking the other day...

about some goofy things that happened during my time in Mother Army. I was stationed in Germany in the mid-1970s. I was the Executive Officer, second in command, of a mechanized rifle battalion. We were stationed at Cooke Barracks in the town of Goeppingen. The battalion had nearly 200 vehicles, tracked and wheeled, in our motor pool. While we had a fence around the motor pool, security was a real issue. The fence had no lights along it, so, after dark, the sentries we posted around the motor pool really couldn't see much that was very far from them.

Vietnam was just over, and the military and its budget were being cut. Try as I might I couldn't get the money approved to get some lights installed around our motor pool. But, you know, perseverance pays off, and, finally, I got the money for the lights. It took a while to get them installed, but the time came and very good lights they were, too.

Problem over? Nope. Now I had to get the extra money to pay for the extra electricity they would use, as they'd be on all night, every night. I never saw that coming, and I never got that money.

For the rest of my 3-year tour we had great lights around our motor pool, but never turned them on.

TAMPA

We left Germany, and I was assigned to USREDCOM (US Readiness Command) located at MacDill AFB in Tampa, FL. My wife, who loves sunshine, thought maybe she'd died and was going to heaven. I spent my four years at USREDCOM in the J-5 (Plans) shop; the first two years I was the war-planner for general war in Europe and back-up planner for war in the Mideast. The final two years I became the primary planner for the Mideast. I was promoted to lieutenant colonel while at MacDill. When my tour was up I was to be assigned to head a ROTC unit somewhere—and ended up at the University of Tampa, so we stayed in Tampa for seven years. Nice.

I was thinking about...

my assignment as a war planner at USREDCOM in Tampa. We war planners shared a large office. Near my desk was a Marine major who was a sharp planner and a great guy. One day he started laughing so loud and so long that the rest of us were drawn to his side. He had just received some kind of weekly or monthly newsletter from Marine Corps Headquarters. Among the articles was a report. The Marines had been quizzing new recruits about why they elected to join the Marines. Many had joined up because of a family tradition. Among the rest the top reason why these young men had joined the Marines was (as I recollect) "I'm tired of everyone telling me what to do; my mother tells me what to do; my coach tells me what to do, etc. I'll show them; I'll join the Marines."

I'm just wondering—did they do a post-basic training survey of how happy these recruits were? I have a funny feeling that they these youngsters didn't get away from being "told what to do."

I was thinking about...

my time at US Readiness Command in Tampa. I was the Middle East war planner. I also had started an on-base Bible study under the cover of the Officers Christian Fellowship (OCF), a group in which I was an active member; I later served on their board. The current board president of the OCF was an active duty Major General, Clay Buckingham. The good general and I were friends. Indeed, we were on a first-name basis; he called me Denny; I, a major, called him General. He was making an official visit to our headquarters, and Marilyn and I invited him to spend the night with us; he accepted.

The next morning we arose, and he and I shared breakfast of cold cereal and milk, along with orange juice. I was eating my cereal and looked into the bowl and saw some bugs—a not uncommon problem in Florida. My problem: what, if anything, to say to the general. I dumped my cereal into the garbage disposal, hoping that if he had the same problem, he'd do the same. He didn't say or do anything but eat his breakfast. To this day I have no idea if, as a good guest in my home, he just ate the bugs, or ate around them, or if his cereal was not infested.

I never had the nerve to ask him.

Here's the rest of the story...

I went to my West Point class' 50th reunion last month. While there I ran into another even older grad also there for his reunion. Retired Major General Clay Buckingham and I were friends when we were on active duty; we were both active in the Officers Christian Fellowship. In the late 1970s I was a major stationed at US Readiness Command in Tampa, and General Buckingham flew into town for a visit at our headquarters. We invited him to stay with us. I normally had cold cereal and orange juice for breakfast; the general said that was fine for him, too. As I was about to eat my cereal I noticed some bugs in the bowl—a not too uncommon situation in Florida. I dumped my cereal in the sink and poured myself some more—no bugs this time. So, what do I do about the General? Tell him about the bugs or wait to see what he did. I stayed quiet. We ate our breakfast and went off to work. I never mentioned this to him—until our chat at West Point last month.

He remembered staying with us, but didn't remember any bugs. We had a good laugh, and now my conscience is clear.

I was thinking back when...

I was assigned to US Readiness Command. The number two guy in the Plans Directorate of our headquarters was a very sharp army one-star general. He was good at giving directions and then leaving planners alone to do their job. Well, the Pentagon had decided to create what we now call US Central Command, and we were given the task of helping create their Plans Directorate. Since Central Command's focus is on the Mideast, of course, I was heavily involved. On one occasion when a number of us, including the general, had been discussing some complex issue, we took a break. When we reassembled, the general said he wanted our advice on a different problem. Of course we paid careful attention.

The general reminded us that a number of 3- and 4-star generals were coming down to get briefed on how we were doing. The general continued that he was, in fact, the only active Army general officer with a mustache. He was, of course, interested in getting his second star, so, he asked us, should he shave off his mustache before the top brass arrived the next week?

To make an understatement, none of us—including this Army major—knew what to say. Was he kidding? If he was serious, why did he think any of us would have any insight on appropriate personal appearance for a brigadier general? He stayed silent. Finally, someone, I think it was me, but this was over 35 years ago, said that his moustache looked fine, certainly was within regulations, and he should probably keep it. Well, he thanked us, and we got back to our original discussions.

For the record, the day the brass showed up—he was clean shaven.

US Army Mustache Regulations

The faces of males shall be clean-shaven while on duty. Mustaches are permitted, but, if worn, shall be neatly trimmed, tidy, and tapered.

Mustaches shall not appear chopped or bushy, and none of the mustache shall cover the upper lip line or extend to the side beyond the corners of the mouth. Beards, handlebar mustaches and goatees are not authorized.

I was thinking about...

a trip I took while I was a war planner at USREDCOM. One of the things our headquarters did regularly was to conduct training exercises around the country, having the different services work together. On one occasion, we had to fly from Florida to the Marine Base at Twenty-Nine Palms, CA. Twenty-Nine Stumps, as it's sometimes called, has a good airfield and lots of land we could use for our exercise. Several Air Force C-141 cargo jets were rigged for passengers and flew our team and our equipment to California. As it turned out, two of our brigadier generals were with us on our aircraft, and the Air Force Wing Commander, another brigadier general, was flying our aircraft. Obviously, the generals hung out together during the long flight across the country. When the time came to land we were, of course, all strapped in. To make an understatement, we hit the ground hard—very, very hard. Indeed, we bounced back up into the air, and hit hard—two more times before we stopped. We were all shaken a bit and glad to be on the ground. It was all worth it when we heard our two generals digging at the flying skills of their friend, our pilot. As it turns out, the aircraft's landing gear was so damaged the plane couldn't be flown out. That was a hard landing.

I was thinking about…

my time as the Mideast war planner at US Readiness Command. While virtually all of the planners and operators in that headquarters were military folks, most of the secretaries and other administrative folks were civilians, and were there for quite a long time. As in most places, if someone comes up with an idea to make things safer or more efficient they can submit the proposal and, if approved, there's a nice cash reward. Well, one of the secretaries was quite bright and knew that all we military folks rotated every 2-4 years. So she wrote up a proposal suggesting that if the outer door to the ladies room swung out, into the hallway instead of into the restroom, it would be safer for the ladies in the restroom. She got an award. Five years later she wrote up another proposal suggesting that if the outer door to the ladies restroom swung in, instead of out into the hallway, then it would be safer for people in the hallway. She got another award. While I was there she again submitted the first proposal, suggesting that the door would be safer if it swung out into the hallway, and again got a cash award. I only knew about all of this because I car-pooled with a couple of secretaries who were laughing about it. Very clever, these civilians.

I was thinking...

about when my tour of duty as a Middle East War Planner at US Readiness Command in Tampa was about up. I was told that I was likely going to be assigned to run a college ROTC department, something I would enjoy. The first college they suggested was Michigan Technical University, which is located on Michigan's upper peninsula, way up north. I didn't know Michigan at all; I'd only been there once, over a decade before, when I took my rifle company to the Detroit riots. We had come to Tampa from Germany, and my wife's only "guidance" to me was to take her where there would be sunshine. So I called the ROTC unit and spoke to a sergeant. After a bit of chit-chat I got to the point. "Sergeant," I asked, "what are summers like up there?" His answer—"Colonel, I'm afraid that I don't know; I overslept that day and totally missed summer." One more instance of a good sergeant telling me clearly what I needed to know. I begged my way out of that assignment. The next offer was one I took—the University of Tampa. We didn't have to move; it was even 5 miles closer to my home than REDCOM was, and yes, I could guarantee sunshine. As we all know, happy wife equals happy life.

The Upper Peninsula

Most people know the state of Michigan is composed of two peninsulas: The lower peninsula is in the shape of a mitten, well populated, with a mixture flatlands and hill with small cities surrounded by farmland.

But the upper peninsula is quite different. It's much colder with only a fraction of the population. (29% of the land area of Michigan but just 3% of its total population)

Winters are long, cold, and snowy, and because of its northern latitude, the daylight hours are short, around 8 hours between sunrise and sunset in the winter. Lake Superior has the greatest effect on the climate, especially the northern and western parts. Lake-effect generates snowfall in excess of 100–250 inches per year.

LATER

*After our seven years in Tampa I was hoping
to join the faculty of the Armed Forces Staff
College at Norfolk, VA. They wanted me,
but there was no current opening in my
rank. I turned down Hawaii and everything
else—I was sure I was going to Norfolk.
One day the phone rang and a captain told
me that I'd waited too long; I was going to
Wyoming, Michigan. I asked him which
state I was being assigned to, Wyoming
or Michigan. It turns out that the City of
Wyoming is a suburb of Grand Rapids, MI.
I became an Army Advisor to the Michigan
Army National Guard. We really didn't want
to go to Michigan, but soon fell in love with
West Michigan. I retired after two years so
they wouldn't move us.*

I was thinking about...

the best advice I ever got when I was on active duty. What came to mind occurred about a year before I retired. We were at Camp Grayling, MI, on National Guard maneuvers and had flown into a headquarters for a briefing that would probably include lunch. I told our chopper pilot, a warrant officer, that he was free until about one pm. My guess was good, so about 12:45 I went to find him. He was checking the aircraft, like a good pilot would do. I told him we'd be done with our meeting and ready to take off at about one. I came back at one and he was still tinkering with the plane. I told him, "Chief, let's go." He looked at me and said, "Colonel, it's far better to be on the ground wishing you were in the air, than…" He didn't finish the sentence—but I got the message. My guidance was, let me know when he and the aircraft were ready to go; he did. We had a safe trip.

I was thinking about...

the time I was in the process of retiring from the Army. I was an Army Advisor to the Michigan Army National Guard. The general who oversaw our activities (my boss' boss) was well, really negative. His comments to guardsmen were often inappropriate, his actions often insulting. And, because the National Guard reports to the governor of the state, the guardsmen could and often did ignore him. We were advisors to the Guard—not their bosses. The general, however, leaned on us, the advisors who did work for him, to get the Guard to comply with his directions. So, when I put in my papers for retirement, I wrote the good general a letter—respectful in tone—that laid out my observations and suggestions on how he might better get compliance from the members of the National Guard. I offered to meet with him to discuss my comments.

As an aside, it was and is common for a soldier who is retiring after a full career in the army to be given an award for meritorious service upon his retirement.

Need I say that the general did not ever acknowledge my letter nor ask to meet with me. And I didn't get an award upon retiring. But I have plenty of awards, it was the right thing to do—and it sure felt good.

I noticed that…

retired Navy Rear Admiral Grace Hopper was being re-membered in the news. Sometime in the late 1970s, as a major, I was sent to a week-long school in Washington DC about using computers; they were the coming thing. One of our lecturers was Grace Hopper. She spoke of being the only female on the team that, during World War II, was creating the computer that would be used to build the atomic bomb. They were building it at the University of Chicago, and the only secure place big enough for them was the space under the stadium seats in the football stadium. They cleaned things up and started putting together vacuum-tubes as they created the computer. She said that the lights in the vacuum tubes attracted all kinds of little critters, the kind that are easy to find under a football stadium. So, a couple of times a week they had to turn everything off, let the tubes cool off, and deal with the mess. As the only woman on the team, she was given the vacuum cleaner; she used it to clean up the dead bodies from around the vacuum-tubes. This, she claimed, was the first de-bugging. There are other stories around about how she became the first person to remove a bug and to call it that, but I heard her tell this story, and I believe it.

She ultimately joined the Navy in 1943. Somewhere along the way she developed the first really useable business computer language called COBAL, or Common Business Oriented Language.

She was an amazing woman, a brilliant naval officer, and a wonderful person. I'll never forget her insights or her stories.

Rear Admiral Grace Hopper

Grace Hopper was born on December 9th, 1906 in New York City and entered the naval reserve in 1943, where she spent most of her career working on computer-related tasks.

Hopper retired from the Naval Reserve at age 60 with the rank of commander. She was recalled to active duty in 1967. She again retired in 1971, but was asked to return to active duty again in 1972. She was promoted to captain in 1973.

She remained on active duty for several years beyond mandatory retirement by special approval of Congress. She retired from the Navy on August 14, 1986 with the rank of rear admiral, lower half. Hopper was awarded the Defense Distinguished Service Medal, the highest non-combat decoration awarded by the Department of Defense. At the time of her retirement, she was the oldest active-duty commissioned officer in the United States Navy. A guided missile destroyer was named for her. USS HOPPER (DDG-70) was commissioned in 1997 and serves today with the US Pacific Fleet.

I was thinking about...

my upcoming 50th reunion at West Point; actually I was thinking about our 40th reunion. When I was a cadet we used what we called "cadet drill." That was the drill that was used by our army during the Revolutionary War. These-days the cadets use standard US Army drill. For our 40th reunion we decided to put together a platoon of about 40 of our class-mates and to do some cadet drill on the parade field during the cadets' Graduation Parade. We were in stands across the field from the brass (the reviewing stand), and we had plenty of room. We were there several days before graduation, so we practiced on the various fields around West Point in our own uniform. We decided that if we asked to do our thing and they said no—well, we were done. So, we just did it. We marched to and onto the field. We acted like we knew what we were doing and were pretty much left alone. We marched out in front of the stands that we and other old grads were in, and did a few moves. Then we turned toward the cadets and the brass and saluted them. Our job done, we moved into the stands to watch the cadets do their thing. The Superintendent, a 3-star general, was very, very unhappy with us, but what could he do? Well, for our 45th reunion, the parade field was fenced off. We couldn't have marched onto the field, and there were more MPs around. We'll likely behave this time, too.

You know the old saying that it's easier to get forgiveness than permission—well, we didn't get either.

West Point Facts

- Established on 16 March 1802
- Motto - Duty, Honor, Country
- Campus - Rural – 16,080 acres
- Cadets - 4,294
- Fight Song - On Brave Old Army Team
- Colors - Black, Gold, and Grey
- Mascot - Black Knight
- Sports - 24 Varsity Teams
- Location - West Point, New York

I've been talking…

to a number of Marines lately, and I was thinking of my funniest, or most fun, time of working with a Marine. I worked with a great Marine for several years, Paul Xavier "PX" Kelly. We met when I was the Mideast war planner at US Readiness Command in Tampa. Our command had recently created Headquarters, Rapid Deployment Joint Task Force, and General Kelly was its first, and only commander. The US Army, Navy, Air Force, and Marines didn't work together very well back in the late 1970s, so the RDJTF's job was to conduct joint exercises to build a cooperative ethic. They also pushed for such things as radios that all services could use so they could talk with each other; at the time, some AF radios wouldn't reach the frequencies that Army forces used, things like that. I like to say that Kelly and I were lieutenants together; you see, he was a new lieutenant general and I was a new lieutenant colonel. We liked each other and got along quite well. He went on to become the Commandant of the Marine Corps.

A number of years later, Bob Dole was running for president. I was the Michigan state chair of Veterans for Dole, and General Kelly was a national spokesman for the campaign.

We were together in Lansing. The next day there was a big Veterans for Dole rally near Detroit; the main speaker was Mrs. Dole. General Kelly was to speak first and then introduce Mrs. Dole. I was to introduce the general. The event was hosted by the Marine Corps League; I'll bet half the people there were Marine vets.

I spoke very positively about General Kelly, an easy thing to do, as he was a great man. I concluded by saying something like this. "General, I really do greatly admire you. While I don't believe in reincarnation, if I did, sir, I just want you to know that if you were reincarnated, you are good enough to come back and be in the Army next time." And the crowd went wild.

West Point's
Cadet Honor Code

"A cadet will not lie, cheat, steal, or tolerate those who do."

I was remembering...

when my wife and I were first married. I had orders to the 101st Airborne Division at Fort Campbell, KY. We rented an apartment off post until we were assigned married quarters on post. As expected, we were assigned to a duplex. We were quite happy with our quarters for the about ten months we were there—before the division deployed to Vietnam in Dec 1967.

About 25 years later, after I'd retired from Mother Army, we were visiting the post as we traveled around a bit. We decided to look for our first house, and we finally found it. We didn't want to bother the folks presently living there, so we just walked around in front and took pictures of each other in the driveway.

It turns out that the officer who was presently living there was in the kitchen talking on the phone, and the kitchen overlooked the driveway. He was talking to his dad, who was a retired army guy. He told his dad about these two old folks looking at the house and taking pictures. His dad told him that we'd likely lived in his quarters at some point—so go invite us in so we could see the place now. He did as his dad suggested, and we got a chance to see our first on-post home. There'd been some very nice modifications since we'd been there. That was a fun visit.

I was thinking about...

a conversation I had with a friend a number of years ago. My friend, Steve, is a college professor in the Social Science Department, so, of course he's a political liberal. I don't remember how our conversation got there, but we ended up talking about security clearances. Steve started laughing and shared a story about a friend of his who goes to his church. Steve's friend was in the Army Reserves and needed to have his security clearance upgraded. He had to provide a number of people the investigators could talk with, and Steve agreed to be available for his friend. One day Steve's phone rang, and it was a very, very serious—and apparently quite young, investigator. He wanted to ask questions about Steve's friend. Steve agreed and answered the many questions. Finally, the young man asked if Steve was aware of anything in his friend's life that caused him concern. Steve said yes, then paused, and noted that his friend has often been seen cavorting with known Republicans. As expected, this really rattled the young investigator's cage. He responded with, "What did you just say?" Steve repeated that his friend does sometimes cavort with known Republicans. At this point, the phone went dead. As an afterthought, the friend did get his clearance. I think you can see why I like hanging out with Steve when I can.

I was talking…

    this past weekend with a lady who works for my Congress-critter. She had a project to try to get a Vietnam veteran an award for heroism that he never received when he was still in the Service. That reminded me of how much effort it was to get valor awards approved, most of the time. When I was a company commander in combat in the 101st Airborne Division I had a great company clerk who took my rough notes and cleaned them up and got things submitted. That worked for many of the awards, but some that I felt were very deserving were disapproved, for whatever reason. I had to find time to re-write and re-submit recommendations along with whatever witness statements I could put together, and this was in the days of typewriters. I got the last batch approved about a year and a half after I'd left command of my company. Many of the troops were then out of the army, but they got their awards. As hard as it was to put together a good awards package only 6 months after the action, it must be really tough 40 years later. I don't know about you, but my memories fade, so accurately recalling something that long ago would be difficult.

    In this case, the vet worked with my friend and eventually received his award.

AFTER THE ARMY

Is there life after the army?

I was thinking about...

When I decided to retire from the Army, I started looking at jobs. A friend from church introduced me to a WWII vet who owned a local company, Behler-Young. Dick Young became my mentor as I looked and evaluated jobs. One day I was talking with him about a decision I was about to make—to enter the manufacturing industry. He interrupted me and asked if I could handle rejection. I said that I could, but asked him what he meant. He told me that his manufacturing division, called Rapid-Line needed a sales engineer, and that he thought I could do the job—but handling rejection is a major factor in sales. I asked Dick if whomever was rejecting my offer could also shoot at me. He said they couldn't. We both laughed and he hired me on the spot. I worked as a sales engineer for the next four years. It was a great job.

I was thinking about...

my son who has always loved soccer. He's now in his mid-40s and still plays and coaches, so after leaving the army, I decided to get involved, too. I became a referee. I ended up doing high school games and AYSO (American Youth Soccer Organization) games. I was ultimately a very senior referee instructor and a national referee for AYSO.

Because my nickname in some places was "the colonel" and it was known that I wouldn't take guff from anyone—I was normally given the games with the most obnoxious coaches.

In Soccer—which is called Football everywhere in the world except the US and Canada (I mean, you do play it with your feet)—one of the sometimes very difficult calls is Off Side. The ref had to be watching the potentially off-side player and hear the kick of the ball and make the decision based on where people were at the moment the ball was played. I still tell people that if you really understand Off Side—get a life. Refs, just make your call and ignore the complaints—I mean, you're going to make half the people angry regardless of what you call (or don't call).

I was thinking about...

how once I was out of the Army for a while, I was often asked to compare and contrast military life to civilian life. My response normally went something like this. Civilians are always a confused mess. Often there is no one in charge. They don't exercise enough, stand up straight, or shine their shoes. Indeed, most of them have never shined the back of their belt-buckles! But, God must love these danged civilians, because He made so many of them. And that is my honest opinion.

I was remembering that…

in the late 70s and early 80s I had been a Middle East War planner and had worked a bit on a plan involving the defense of Saudi Arabia. When Saddam's Iraq invaded Kuwait and threatened to continue his attack south into Saudi Arabia (he never did that), the US military put together a plan which became known as Desert Shield. While the plan I'd written was to defend Saudi Arabia from a Soviet attack, Iran was using Russian equipment and tactics, so it worked pretty well. I had been making myself available to various local media as a military specialist, so I was known a bit. Well, when Desert Shield began, I suddenly became quite popular. And when the ground attack phase of Desert Storm began (it only lasted 100 hours before Iraq surrendered) I was really popular. Then military things slowed down a bit.

Then came 9-11 and I got a few phone calls.

My favorite radio station, WOOD Radio in Grand Rapids, MI, was my most frequent interviewer—four or five times a year.

Then one of the part time employees at WOOD graduated from college and joined the Air Force—of course he left WOOD. A few years later Josh Leng came back from the

Air Force and went back to work for WOOD. He told the management that WOOD should have a military talk radio show—and they listened. Then he was asked who the host would be, Josh said he'd ask Denny Gillem (we knew each other through church and some political activities). So, the way Frontlines of Freedom began was when Josh called me up and said, "Denny, would you like to host a military talk-radio show on WOOD?" An old friend of mine who is an evangelist likes to say, "let me pray about that....Amen, okay." So that's what I said.

Most radio shows are begun by people with a vision who work for months and years putting ideas together and then selling the idea to both stations and potential sponsors. All I had to do was say, "Let me pray about that.....Amen; ok."

I was remembering that...

on one occasion while I was hosting *Frontlines of Freedom*, I had an interview with a 4-star admiral who was the Vice Chief of Naval Operations. We had a good talk about our navy. As we were wrapping up our interview, I made a final comment. I knew that he was a Naval Academy grad, so after thanking him for being my guest, I said, of course, "Beat Navy, sir!" His response took me out. He said, "Not this year, Denny." And he was right, Army got creamed that year. We closed the interview with both of us laughing.

I was remembering that...

on another occasion I had a long-sought interview with a very sharp member of Congress. After scheduling and re-scheduling, he was finally available—but even on that day we had to delay the interview by an hour or so—but finally the phone rang and he was ready. It was a 20 minute interview and it went perfectly—we just clicked. Then I thanked him and said good-bye and hung up. And then I noticed that I'd forgotten to turn on the recorder. I'm still kicking myself on that one. And, no, I haven't yet been able to get him back—but I'm working on it.

I think it's clear

that I've lived a very blessed life. I don't remember ever wanting to be anything else but a soldier. Okay, it took three tries before I got into West Point, but I made it. West Point took my strengths, weaknesses, goals, and dreams and molded me into a man. Airborne and Ranger Schools put on some of the final touches--before I went out to meet the real world. It was my good fortune to work with a lot of great sergeants and some fine officers who, one way or another, helped me grow and mature. I truly loved being in the Army. In the almost 30 years since I retired I have seen that the old saying "you can take the boy out of the Army, but you can't take the Army out of the boy" is very true – at least in me. I've worked in a variety of sales and management and education positions over the years and have done pretty well. I've been politically active; I even ran for public office twice – and came in second twice. I still believe that my oath to support and defend the Constitution of the United States is active and valid. It really bothers me when I see politicians ignore that special document; it bothers me that most Americans have never read it. So, I teach American Government part-time at the local Community College and host *Frontlines of Freedom*. I love America and my family and my God. I am the Smiling Ranger; I smile because I'm happy.

– Denny Gillem

Lieutenant Colonel Denny Gillem is a West Point graduate and a Vietnam combat veteran. He served two tours in Vietnam as a company grade officer where he received seven US awards for valor. After a distinguished military career, he retired and now lives in Michigan as a college professor and the host of Frontlines of Freedom, the nation's number one military and veteran radio show.

You can listen to Denny every weekend by visiting www.frontlinesoffreedom.com.